A History of

IOWA WINE

Vines on the Prairie

John N. Peragine

Published by American Palate
A Division of The History Press
Charleston, SC
www.historypress.com

First published 2019

Manufactured in the United States

ISBN 9781467141086

Library of Congress Control Number: 2018966322

To my wife, Kate, and my children, Max, Loreena and Sarah,
for tolerating my dreams of wine and writing.

CONTENTS

Acknowledgements 9
Introduction 11

1. The L'oste Vineyard 15
2. Keokuk and Black Hawk 22
3. White Elk Winery 31
4. Council Bluffs Grape Growers Association 44
5. Amana Colonies: Ten Wineries 63
6. Challenges of Growing in Iowa 92
7. Vineyard Revival 101

Bibliography 119
Index 123
About the Author 125

ACKNOWLEDGEMENTS

I could not have made this book without the help of the Iowa Wine Growers Association, Iowa State University, the Amana Heritage Association, Backcountry Winery, Summerset Winery, Ackerman Winery and Tassel Ridge Winery.

Some special acknowledgements are due to Michael White, Tom Gardner, Linda Ackerman, Cassie Bott, Peter Hoehnle, Rebecca Dickman, Katie Reinhardt, Tonya Bolt, Amber Gable, Bob Wersen, Deb Hamilton, Clayton Walker, Michael DeCapria, Chad Rhoad, Hilary Parrish and Gena Schantz.

INTRODUCTION

In 2015, when I stepped onto a porch awaiting my real estate agent, little did I know I was looking at history and my own destiny. The house was on a high bluff in Davenport, Iowa, and overlooked the Mississippi River to the south. In the distance past the bridge and barges I could see Rock Island, Illinois.

It had just rained, and there was a rainbow in the sky that seemed to touch down at the bottom of the property. It was a sign. The backyard was overgrown with trees of heaven and weeds, but it was obvious it was tiered. I looked to the left and there were two houses that looked like the one I was considering buying, and the tiers seemed to match up to those in the yard below. To my right was a large Italianate home with Greek Revival features. The all-white structure was two stories tall with large columns.

The real estate agent arrived. The house was everything my wife and I were looking for, and I joked that maybe I could clean up the jungle below the house and fulfill my dream of building a vineyard. I had been making wine at home for fifteen years but had never grown any grapes.

Before we purchased the house, my mother-in-law, Gena Schantz, came to look at the property and was very excited because she knew of its history. She is the foremost authority on George Davenport, the founder for whom the town is named. The large home next door was once owned by his only son, George L'oste Davenport. With a little digging in her notes, Gena found the explanation for the tiered property that ran through our house and those next to us. It was once one large vineyard of six thousand vines. It was my dream almost realized. I had the property but not the vineyard.

Catawba grapevine in spring 2018, at the L'oste Winery in Davenport, Iowa. The bluff is south facing and overlooks the Mississippi River, with the state of Illinois on the other side. *Author's collection.*

The L'oste Vineyard was planted on the site of the Clifton vineyard in Davenport in 2017. There were 140 vines planted, including Catawba grapes, which were originally planted by George L'oste Davenport in the later 1800s. *Author's collection.*

Later that year, I met with George Walker, who owns a winery, Mountain Vista Winery, in Rancho Cucamonga, California. He wanted to write a book about the history of the area related to winemaking, and so we brokered a deal. I would help him write the book, and he would build me a vineyard.

The book, *Cucamonga Valley Wine: The Lost Empire of American Winemaking* (2017, The History Press), was completed, and in 2017, George's son Clayton came and over eight days built the vineyard of 139 vines. We received some local press, so we had to come up with a name for the vineyard. We took George's middle name and did a little play on words: the L'oste Vineyard was named because it was truly a vineyard that was lost in history and has now been found.

Katie Reinhardt, the special collections librarian at the Davenport Public Library, wrote a blog in response to the article about the vineyard, which inspired me to look further into the history of wine in Iowa. What I found was amazing; before there was corn, there were grapes, and they were plentiful. The rich history of Iowa's viniculture has been lost for many years, but in the last decade, there has been a resurgence in the number of vineyards in Iowa. In order to predict the future, we must look to the past, and the challenges of one hundred years ago to grow grapes in the Midwest are not much different than they are today.

It is my hope that you, the reader, will find some fascinating tidbits of wine history in this book and that they inspire you to try some of the wonderful wines available. It is also my hope that we learn to preserve our heritage, protect our lands and use technology to grow wonderful grapes while at the same time saving our environment.

Some of the sections of this book would not have been possible without the contributions of some key people. The section on the White Elk Vineyard came from Tom Gardner's *Wine in Keokuk: Now and Then*. Tom provided some wonderful images and stories of Hiram Barney and Chief Keokuk. The section about wine history comes from the work of Peter Hoehle and a whitepaper he was commissioned to create for the Ackerman Winery and used with generous permission by Cassie Bott.

Gena Schantz's thirty-plus years of research into George Davenport were pivotal in my research about him and the Clifton Vineyard.

Chapter 1

THE L'OSTE VINEYARD

It seems only right to begin the journey of the history of wine by beginning with George L. Davenport's vineyard.

The Clifton House was built in 1853 by J.M.D. Burrows, who had arrived at the town of Davenport in 1838 and built a wholesale company, Burrows and Prettyman. The name "Clifton" was given to the house because it overlooked a high bluff, and local lore says that Burrows built his home to overlook the Mississippi River and watch his profits coming up the river. He did business along the Upper Mississippi River and west to the Missouri River in Iowa and Nebraska.

The bulk of Burrows's profits came from contracts he had with the U.S. government to supply Fort Crawford and Fort Snelling along the Mississippi River. Everything was grand until the bottom fell out of the financial markets in the Panic of 1857. Burrows was forced to mortgage his house to Antoine LeClaire, who was one of the major players in the development of the Quad Cities and surrounding areas. (There is a town named LeClaire up the river from Davenport.)

Burrows used the proceeds from the mortgage to pay off his debts, but he was never able to get ahead and was never able to gain back the title to the Clifton House. The house was sold to George L'oste Davenport, who was the son of George Davenport, one of the original settlers in the area and after whom the town is named.

Davenport's sisters lived in the home for twenty-five years, during which time Clifton Vineyard was built. It stood vacant for another twenty-five

Close-up of the Clifton manor. In the early 1900s, a second floor was built where the upper terraces were, and where the group of trees is on the left is where a house was built where the author currently resides and has replanted some of the vineyard, now named the L'oste Vineyard. *A.T. Andreas'* Illustrated Historical Atlas of the State of Iowa.

years. The house was then sold in 1905 to John Winter, who converted it into apartments. Three houses were built beside it, one of which I now live in.

The Clifton House looks very different than it did when it was built. The house was built in the Italianate style with elements of Greek Revival and has large Renaissance Ionic columns that hold up the portico. It has a large square cupola on the center of a hipped roof. It has five narrow, round arched windows on each side of the house. The columns are on paneled pedestals, and there is a concrete balustrade that was extended during its renovation in the twentieth century. There is a one-story porch on the north side that once extended the length of the house.

The original shape of the house was of a three-tiered cake, and the upper part was a tower room with windows on four sides. Local legend is that the tower was for watching for escaped slaves making their way northward via a barge during the days of the Underground Railroad.

The house was originally one story, with two bay wings on the east and west sides as they are in the image above. When the house was renovated after 1905, the porches were eliminated, and a second floor was added on both wings and became apartments. John Winter had loved the house from his childhood, which is why he had bought it. He did not want to change it too drastically, and he left the twelve-foot ceilings, crystal chandeliers, coal-burning fireplaces and massive mahogany fireplaces.

The Clifton House was the setting for the novel *The Man of the Hour* by Davenport native Alice French (better known as Octave Thanet).

GEORGE DAVENPORT

George Davenport was an important figure in Iowa and American history. He was born John King in 1783 in Louth, Lincolnshire, England. Historians are unsure why he changed his name. However, changing names upon coming to America was a common practice during this time. During his lifetime of adventure, he was a tailor, sailor, frontiersman, fur trader, merchant, postmaster, U.S. Army soldier, Indian agent and eventually a city planner.

Davenport was apprenticed to a tailor in Louth, Lincolnshire, but later was placed with an uncle on a merchant ship. As part of the crew, he visited many ports in France and Spain and on the Baltic. His final voyage brought him to New York. During a daring rescue of a fellow sailor who fell overboard, Davenport seriously injured his leg. He stayed in the United States to recover and was recruited into the United States Army. He served for ten years, during which time he fought in the War of 1812 under General James Wilkinson. In 1813, at the end of the Peoria War, he escorted the Pottawatomie delegation to St. Louis to sign a peace treaty. In attendance of the treaty were Black Partridge, Senachwine, Comas, Shick Shack, Crow and Gomo.

In 1815, George Davenport was discharged from the army and was hired by a government contractor to supply the army, which was then establishing forts deep in Indian country on the Upper Mississippi River. Davenport settled near Fort Armstrong, which was near Rock Island, and traded with local tribes in the Illinois and Iowa territories.

George Davenport established several trading posts, but his main post was on Rock Island. He contracted as an agent of the American Fur Company and partnered with Russell Farnham, a pioneer and fur trader. The two established a trading center on the mainland near Fort Armstrong, around which became a small settlement locally known as Farnhamsburg. That area is now incorporated into modern-day Rock Island, Illinois. In 1825, Davenport became the postmaster of Rock Island.

Davenport married widow Margaret Bowling Lewis, who was fourteen years his senior. Davenport's sons were born to Susan Lewis, who was Margaret Lewis's daughter. Firstborn son George L'oste was born on the island in 1817. A second son, Bailey, was born in 1823 in Cincinnati. Bailey Davenport was interested in agriculture, especially focusing on horse breeding. He operated several businesses in coal, sand and gravel and was elected mayor of Rock Island during the Civil War. Davenport also had a daughter, Elizabeth, born to Catherine, who had been a housekeeper for the Davenports. George and Catherine never married.

After living with his family in a double log cabin for many years, Davenport built a fine home on the island of Rock Island (now called Government Island) near Fort Armstrong. In 1835, he partnered with six other investors, including Antoine LeClaire, to develop a town called Davenport in his honor.

Davenport retired from the American Fur Company and the Indian trade business in 1842. During his retirement, he invested in land in many of the towns that now form the Quad Cities and developed businesses that his sons would later continue.

On July 4, 1845, Davenport's family was celebrating Independence Day when a group of bandits entered their home. Davenport, who had stayed home that day, was attacked and later died of his injuries. Edward Bonney, a detective and bounty hunter, was hired to pursue the assailants of Davenport and was credited with arresting many of the band. The men were tried and convicted of murder. Three men—Granville Young, John Young and Aaron Young—were hanged on the town square for the crime.

George L'oste Davenport

George L'oste Davenport was born on November 17, 1817, on Rock Island. He grew up with Meskwaki children as his playmates and was able to learn how to speak Ho Chunk, Sauk and Meskwaki; he was even adopted into the tribe and named Musquake.

George L'oste Davenport was educated in Jacksonville, Illinois. When he returned home, he became a partner in his father's Indian trading business and the mercantile business owned by his father and Antoine LeClaire in Davenport, Iowa.

As he grew older, he became active in city developments. He was one of the town's first trustees and was elected alderman of the Fourth Ward from 1861 to 1865. He was involved in several other businesses, such as the manufacture of flour, and even owned a distillery with his cousin James Bowling. He helped organize the Mississippi and Missouri Railroad Company.

George L'oste continued to work with his father's friend Antoine LeClaire in building a foundry and machine shop. He served as president of the first gas company in Davenport and owned blocks of shops. It all came crashing down in the 1870s, and he suffered financial ruin.

The following is from the *Annals of Iowa*, 1863:

> *Burrows & Prettyman had their mill in operation in a few days after that of Mr. Fulton's, and Davenport, which before had never possessed a mill of any kind, now sent up the steam from two first rate flouring mills, while one could have done the business and was amply sufficient, as was afterwards shown. Mr. Fulton ran his mill about a year and failed. It was then rented to G.L. Davenport, Wm. Inslee and L.A. Macklot, who ran it a year and a half, and lost some three thousand dollars in the operation, when it was sold to Burrows & Prettyman for the sum of ten thousand five hundred dollars, who ran it a year, lost money, and then used it two years as a warehouse. The machinery was then sold to parties in Le Claire and was consumed by fire a few years since. The building was torn down to give room for the block of stores built by Mr. Burrows in 1855.*

THE CLIFTON VINEYARD

In the *Report of the Secretary of the Iowa State Agricultural Society of 1870* by William K. Haight, he describes the Clifton Vineyard:

> *The season has been particularly favorable for grapes, and every person so fortunate as to possess a single bearing vine has had a rich reward for his expenditures in this luscious fruit.*
>
> *The vintage has been unusually large and of superior quality for wine making. George L. Davenport, the fortunate possessor of Clifton vineyard, has six thousand vines in bearing, and the present year has made two thousand gallons of wine, expressing the juice by a machine of his own invention, which picks the grapes from the stems, and performs all the operations without the necessity of using the wine press. He uses twelve pounds of grapes for a gallon of wine, racks it off by Christmas, adds sugar as it needs, and bottles in clear March weather, when the wine is between two and three years old. He has on hand twelve thousand bottles of old wine.*
>
> *...Mr. Davenport considers the Catawba grape superior to any for wine.*

George L'oste's was not the only vineyard, nor the largest. According to Haight's report:

Above: Clifton Vineyard, owned by George L'oste Davenport. There were over six thousand vines of Catawba grapes planted, circa 1875. *A.T. Andreas'* Illustrated Historical Atlas of the State of Iowa.

Left: George L'oste Davenport was the only son of George Davenport, one of the founders of the Quad Cities for whom the town of Davenport is named. The Clifton home was acquired through a bank sale. Banditti of the Prairie, *Edward Bonnie.*

> *At the Black Hawk Vineyards, the property of Messrs. A. & F. Schmidt, all the appliances for making wine on a large scale are found. Nine thousand gallons were made the present season, using over one hundred thousand pounds of their grapes of their own raising. They rack off their wine several times the first winter, and bottle the spring, or summer following. A large proportion of their wines are sold by the barrel. So great has been the demand for their production that they have on hand but five hundred gallons of old wine—mostly of 1869. They consider the quality of the present vintage superior to the average and think the year 1870 will long be remembered as the great wine year.*
>
> *...Messrs. Schemidt give preference to the Delaware for white wine, and Norton's Virginia for red wine.*

In 1879, George L'oste was appointed the Indian agent for the Meskwaki. He went to St. Augustine, Florida, for health reasons and died there on February 27, 1885. However, the wine industry had taken hold in the Davenport area.

The *Des Moines Register* reported on October 11, 1890, "Large shipments of grapes are being made from the Iowa 'grape belt' through Davenport to the northern market. The Fruit is of excellent quality and brings 3½ cents per pound."

Chapter 2

KEOKUK AND BLACK HAWK

The history of wine in America spans all the way back to 1620, when writers of that era talked about making wines from native vines in the eastern United States. Sir John Hawkins wrote that wine was made in Florida as early as 1564. In 1620, a vineyard was established in Virginia. By 1652, there were premiums offered for those wanting to produce wine in Virginia. In 1664, Paul Richards planted a vineyard near New York. In Philadelphia, there were attempts to build vineyards in 1683 and 1685, but these failed. More attempts were made in New Jersey with some more success, but all of these were experiments. It was not until the early nineteenth century that vineyards began to be built in earnest and flourish. But the Midwest was still the frontier, and it took several years before vineyards were built commercially.

These first vineyards were small, only about five acres on average, and unfortunately, many failed because foreign grapes were planted, which were not suited for the cold climate. Those who planted native varieties had more success, and it would be many years before hybrids that are used today were developed. The wineries that were the most successful in early American wine history were in North and South Carolina, where the scuppernong, a native vine, was king.

As the frontier moved west, so did attempts at producing wine. In the late 1700s, travel writer Constantin Francois de Chasseboeuf, comte de Volney, simply known as Volney, wrote that he *tasted wine made from native grapes at Gallipolis, Ohio, in 1796, and Dufour, in 1799, found a Frenchman at Marietta, Ohio, who made a few barrels of wine every year from grapes collected in the woods, equal to the wine made in several parts of the United States that I visited in 1794, were found worthy the name of vineyards.*

I went to see all the vines growing that I could hear of, even as far as Kaskaskia, on the Mississippi, where I was informed the Jesuits had planted a vineyard shortly after the first settlement of the country, but that the French government had ordered it to be destroyed, for fear that vine culture might spread in America and hurt the wine trade of France. I found only the spot where that vineyard had been planted, in a well-selected place on the side of a hill, under a cliff to the northeast of the town. No good grapes were found there or in any gardens of the country.

In 1860, the eighth census of the U.S. government says this about viticulture in the United States:

Vineyard culture in the United States may now be considered as fairly established. Wine is made in thirty of the thirty four States of the Union, of different qualities of course, and with varied success. As to its future production in quantity, I should name, first California; second, the mountainous districts of the southern States, as most favorable on account of the climate; third, the Ohio and Mississippi valleys; fourth, the middle States; and last, the eastern. As to quality, the best samples have been found in Georgia and the Ohio valley.

The impression is that in the middle and eastern States the climate is too cold to elaborate sufficient saccharine matter in the grape to make a wine that will keep without the addition of sugar. But this may prove a mistake—new varieties may yet be produced to suit each section of our country where the grape is grown. They are now numbered by hundreds, and new hybrids are annually added to the lists.

After all our experience during the last seventy years, vine culture in the United States is but yet in its infancy, and we have much to learn. The few millions of gallons which we produce annually, are as nothing when compared to the nine hundred millions of France, or the three thousand million of all Europe. The vineyards of Europe are estimated at twelve millions of acres. We have far more grape territory than that in the United States; but our climate, with the exception of California, is less equable. In California alone, it is stated, there are five millions of acres well adapted to grape culture. Here is something to reflect upon, and to give hope for the future.

It was not until about 1857 that grape growing as a commercial proposition began to take hold. It began in the western part of Iowa. In 1869, White Elk Vineyards in Keokuk, Iowa, began producing grapes and wine. In a letter included in the *Grape Culturist: A Monthly Journal Devoted to Grape Culture and Wine-Making*, A.S. Bonham asked about the potential prices for Concord wine he was planning on producing from the 1869 crop:

July 11, 1869 Council Bluffs, Iowa. Geo Husmann Esq.:
Dear Sir
I have your work on Grape Culture and the Manufacture of American Wines, and I value it very highly indeed. And, as I have grown the grapes and want to press the juice this fall, I want to ask you a few more questions, for fear I should make a mistake. I have three acres now in bearing, the third crop, and they are fine and healthy—mostly Concord. I have set five acres more this spring, and intend to plant five more, making thirteen acres in all; and I want to ask you if pine will answer for fermenting casks as well as oak; or would I, through you have such casks shipped from your place, or St. Louis, as you think I will need for the present crop. I would like at least one or two 500-gallon casks furnished by you of oak, the balance I could get here. If you can furnish them please give me the probable cost, delivered here by boat or rail. Please say whether I could get along without the must scale, and if not, where I can obtain them best. I also want a press and am not able to buy any larger one than will answer my purpose; please say where I can do the best, and what you think I can wholesale the wine at next March, if good. Please answer the above; and if you can furnish the casks I will send you the money. I would be pleased to have any suggestions you will be pleased to make.
Very truly yours,
A.S. Bonham

[We do not trade in casks, but you cannot do better than by addressing Mr. Tobias Weigold, whose address you will find in our advertising columns. He has furnished us with casks for years, and they have always given satisfaction. Pine will not do to keep wine in for a longer time than a few days.…You cannot do without the must scale. By addressing Jacob Blattner, St. Louis, and sending $3.50, can obtain one. The press of Geiss

& Brosius., Belleville, Ills., will answer your purpose, price $45. The price of new Concord wine at wholesale last fall has been from 80c to $1 at Hermann; of course we cannot tell what it may be worth with you next spring. It depends on the quality, and the market you have.—Ed.]

THE HALF-BREED TRACT

Hiram Barney, a slick city attorney from New York, made his first trip to Keokuk, Iowa, in 1841. The purpose of his trip was to acquire land for his clients under the half-breed program, which provided tracts of land set aside by the government for the children of mixed European and Native American ancestry.

Carte de visite (a visiting or calling card was popular in the mid- to late 1800s) of Hiram Barney, named the "White Elk" by Chief Keokuk's tribe. Hiram obtained land through President Lincoln's "half-breed program," which he later deeded to his son, Lewis Barney, and used to create the White Elk Winery. *Tom Gardner Collection.*

The half-breed tract in Iowa was located in Lee County and contained approximately 119,000 acres between the Mississippi and Des Moines Rivers. It was a part of the treaty between the Sauk people, the Fox tribe and the United States government. There were many problems with the half-breed tracts, including claims by people who never lived on the tracts and resold the land to land speculators.

Joseph Smith Jr., the Mormon leader, purchased half-breed tracts in Iowa in 1837 through a land speculation company. There were problems with the deeds, and much of the land purchased could not be held except for about one thousand acres that included the town of Commerce, Illinois. This land was important, as it was where members of the Mormon Church fled when they were driven from Missouri due to Missouri Executive Order 44, which was issued by Governor Lilburn Boggs. The order was the result of a clash between the Latter-day Saints and the Missouri State Militia. The declaration stated, "The Mormons must be treated as enemies, and must be exterminated or driven from the State if necessary for the public peace—through outrages are beyond all description."

There were a number of opportunists from the East looking to acquire land for pennies on the dollar from people who had no concept of owning land. People were acquiring and selling land through the half-breed tract program through dubious means.

Hiram Barney was looking specifically for land on which to build a vineyard because he was convinced that particular area of the Mississippi River Valley was capable of producing world-class wines. Hiram had exchanged letters with a friend of his from college, David W. Kilbourne, who described a vineyard he had planted with Isaac Galland in the town of Keokuk just a few years earlier.

The New York Land Company hired attorneys like Hiram Barney and the famous Francis Scott Key to help in the land grab. There were Iowa territory agents such as Isaac Campbell and David W. Kilbourne who assisted in the land speculation. The territorial legislature passed a law that allowed settlers to occupy the land until all the legal issues had been worked out. The New York Land Company obtained a decree from the district court that allowed the land to be divided among 101 property owners. Barney saw an opportunity to obtain the land for his vineyard, which is what prompted his trip to Keokuk in October 1841. It was not enough for Hiram to just buy a tract of land in hopes the issues would be worked out legally; he wanted to strengthen his claim to his title of the land, and there was but one way to do that.

CHIEF KEOKUK

Keokuk was the chief of the Sauk tribe, although he was not actually a chief by birth. He was regarded as a great orator and was responsible for the conflict between the Sauk and the United States government that led to the Black Hawk War.

In a treaty of 1804, the United States negotiated the sale of lands east of the Mississippi occupied by the Sauk and Meskwaki tribes. It was said the purchase price was $2,200 in goods and an annual payment of $1,000 of goods. The problem was that those tribal leaders who signed the treaty were not authorized to do so.

The Sauk were allowed to live on their ceded lands and lived in their primary village, Saukenuk, where the Mississippi and Rock Rivers converge. In 1828, the U.S. government began surveying the land for white settlement, and the Sauk were told by Indian agent Thomas Forsyth to vacate Saukenuk.

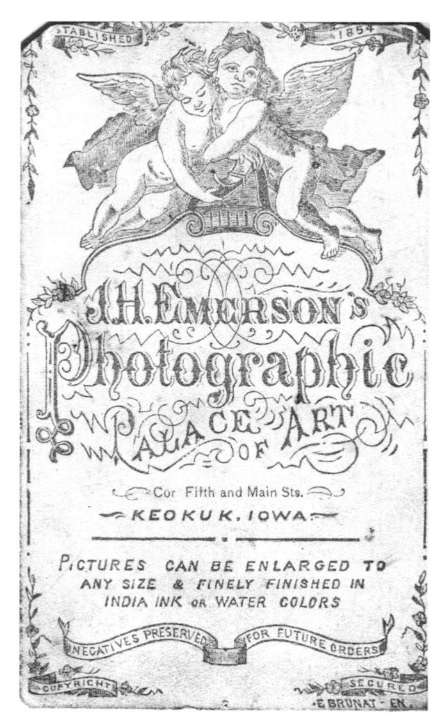

Left: Carte de visite of Chief Keokuk. The federal government made Keokuk the principal chief of the Sauk and Fox Indians after the Black Hawk War and required the tribes to move into Iowa, near their agency. This was where Hiram Barney found Keokuk, who called Barney "White Elk." Barney used this name for his vineyard. *Tom Gardner Collection.*

Right: The carte de visite of Chief Keokuk was made in the photographic studio of J.H. Emerson of Keokuk, Iowa. This is a copy of Thomas Easterley's daguerreotype, circa 1880. *Tom Gardner Collection.*

Many of the Sauk, while disputing the 1804 treaty, did not want to get into a conflict with the U.S. government and decided it was best to move west of the Mississippi. The leader of this group was Keokuk. Even though he thought the 1804 treaty was a fraud, he had participated in the War of 1812 to defend Saukenuk against the United States. He had been in the East and had seen the size of the cities and manpower of the U.S. Army. He felt it would be foolish to resist them.

Black Hawk, another tribal leader of the Sauk but not a civil chief, returned to Saukenuk after a winter hunting party and found white settlers who were there in anticipation of the land being given over to them. Black Hawk and his party got into clashes with the settlers but then left the village on another hunting trip.

Keokuk assured Forsyth that the Sauk would not return to Saukenuk. Black Hawk did not agree and returned in the spring of 1830 with two hundred Kickapoo, an ally of the Sauk, to take back their village. Black Hawk and his men became known as the "British Band" because they would often raise a British flag in defiance of claims of United States sovereignty over their land. They also hoped to gain allies of the British stationed in Fort Maiden in Canada.

July 15, 1830, marks the day the U.S. Indian commissioner William Clark signed a treaty with the Sauk and Fox tribes that ceded over twenty-six million acres of land east of the Mississippi to the U.S. government. It provided a neutral zone between the Sauk and Fox tribes from their sworn enemies, the Sioux. Keokuk signed the treaty as a representative of the Sauk and Fox, and it was approved by the Dakota Sioux.

In 1831, Black Hawk returned. This time, the British Band had grown to 1,500 with the addition of members of the Potawatomi tribe. The conflict continued. The United States Army had no cavalry to pursue the Sauk should they flee, so Illinois governor John Reynolds gathered 1,500 members of the volunteer militia.

Keokuk, who had become a rival of Black Hawk, convinced many of his band to give up the fight and leave Illinois. General Edmund P. Gaines, commander of the Western Department of the United States Army, launched an assault on Saukenuk on June 30, 1831, to finally drive out Black Hawk and his followers. When they arrived, the village was empty, as Black Hawk and his band had retreated to the western side of the Mississippi. A treaty was finally signed by Black Hawk and other leaders with Gaines stating that the Sauks would remain on the western side of the Mississippi and that the tribes would break off contact with the British in Canada.

Even though Black Hawk had signed the treaty, he did not stay on the western side of the Mississippi for long. Black Hawk received bad information from Sauk civil chief Neapope that the British and other tribes were in support of the Sauk taking back their land. According to Neapope, a shaman named Wabokiesheik, known as the Winnebago Prophet, had stated that their tribes were ready to support Black Hawk. Even though Black Hawk found the information to be less than accurate, he did decide to return to the Illinois side of the Mississippi River with five hundred warriors and about six hundred noncombatants. Instead of going to Saukenuk, the group went to Prophetstown, which was the name of Wabokiesheik's village, about thirty-five miles north of Saukenuk.

General Henry Atkinson was tasked with stopping further conflict in the region. Keokuk, Atkinson and Meskwaki chief Wapello had been trying to get Black Hawk to turn back from his push up the Rock River. Because the support of the other tribes was not as promised and without the support of the British, Brigadier Black Hawk was ready to negotiate with Atkinson.

Before that could happen, an encounter with Illinois militiamen turned the tide of war. Two battalions of untrained militia under the charge of Major Isaiah Stillman were sent to scout out the British Band. This proved to be a mistake. Black Hawk sent three warriors with a flag of truce to parley. At this point, he did not want an armed conflict.

The militia grabbed the group and opened fire on Black Hawk's band. Black Hawk's warriors beat the battalion, with twelve militiamen losing their life. Black Hawk only lost three warriors at the Battle of Stillman's Run, but it set the stage for a greater conflict. President Jackson and Lewis Cass, the secretary of war, were no longer interested in diplomatic solutions with Black Hawk and the British Band; they wanted to crush them as a warning to other tribes rising up against the United States government.

Militias were sent out to find Black Hawk and his band. Black Hawk went north to Lake Koshkonog in the Michigan territory and secured a safe place for the women, children and other noncombatants to stay. He had picked up some allies from the Ho-Chunk and Potawatomi tribes, and they went on raids of white settlements. One of the raids, the Indian Creek Massacre, resulted in the killing and scalping of fifteen men, women and children.

Atkinson and other militia leaders had difficulty keeping their battalions together and focused. Atkinson began recruiting Native American allies of the Menominees, Dakotas and Ho-Chunks. The allies were placed under the command of William S. Hamilton, son of Alexander Hamilton, but they lost interest and began fighting the war on their own terms.

The war continued. President Andrew Jackson was not happy with the results and placed the command under General William Scott. Many of Scott's men became sick or died of cholera on their way to the Midwest. In the meantime, Atkinson wanted to end the conflict with his militiamen before the regulars arrived.

The Battle of Wisconsin Heights turned the war back in favor of the militia, with 68 of Black Hawk's warriors killed. After the battle, Scott's army arrived, and the force grew to 900 militiamen and 400 regulars compared to Black Hawk's British Band that had been reduced to 260 warriors.

The army caught up with Black Hawk's band at the mouth of the Bad Ax River. The military had a steamboat equipped with large guns. Black Hawk tried to surrender, but the military was not interested in a parley and opened fire on the warriors. Twenty-three more of Black Hawk's men fell.

The war was over. The final death count of settlers, regular soldiers and militiamen was seventy-seven, while the British Band had lost upward of six hundred men. Black Hawk had escaped but was later turned in for a $100 bounty. He was imprisoned and moved to a couple of forts. He was eventually released, but there was a condition that he had to visit large eastern cities to experience the might of the United States in order to dissuade the tribes from rising up again.

In 1832, there was a treaty with the Sauk and Meskwaki, with Keokuk and Wapello as representatives of the tribes. The tribes sold six million acres in eastern Iowa to the United States for $20,000 a year for thirty years. Keokuk was given a reservation in the cession and became the recognized leader of the Sauk and Meskwaki.

Chapter 3

WHITE ELK WINERY

Hiram Barney knew that the one sure way to secure his title to the land in Keokuk was to visit the chief himself and somehow become a member of the tribe. Keokuk was living in Agency, Iowa, where he resided as the Indian agent for the Sauk and Meskwaki. For Barney, this was a 130-mile trip through rough terrain, open prairies and roads that in places were nothing more than goat paths. Barney was determined to meet with Keokuk and be adopted into the Sauk tribe. When he arrived at Keokuk's camp, the chief and lesser chiefs met him with open arms and celebrated Barney's arrival with great reverence. The ceremony and celebration lasted for many days

At some point during the celebration, Barney made his request to Keokuk. The chief did not answer right away and asked for some time to consider his proposal. When the celebration ended and it was time for Barney to make the long trek back home, Keokuk was not in attendance to see him off.

However, Barney's party had not traveled far before Na-She-Kus-Kuk, a lesser chief, intercepted the party with fifty mounted warriors. The chief reported to Barney that Keokuk had sent him to perform the ceremony of tribal adoption. Barney was very pleased that his efforts had been rewarded and expressed his deep appreciation to Na-She-Kus-Kuk, at which point the chief raised his hands and uttered the name "Wa-Be-Me-Shi-Wa"—Hiram Barney's new tribal name. The word roughly translates to "White Elk." It is eventually what Barney was to name his vineyard, but it would not become a reality until the late 1860s, twenty-five years later.

Barney returned to New York City, where he raised a family and concentrated on building up his law practice. He and his wife, Susan, had six children, and Barney's wealth and influence grew. He was committed to the abolition of slavery and was nominated for a seat in Congress by the Anti-Slavery Party in 1840. He also served as a presidential elector for the Free Soil Party in 1848. Hiram continued his political involvement in 1856 when he became a delegate for the first Republican National Convention as a supporter of Charles Sumner. Unfortunately for Barney and Sumner, John C. Frémont won the nomination. In 1860, Barney supported Salmon P. Chase.

In that same year, Abraham Lincoln came to New York to give his famous Cooper Union speech. Barney attended and was so impressed that he took Lincoln out to dinner at the Athenaeum Club on Fifth Avenue. By the time the Republican National Convention began in Chicago, Barney had switched his support from Chase to Lincoln. He knew that Chase would not be nominated, and after the convention, he helped raise $35,000 for Lincoln's presidential campaign.

Lincoln seemed very impressed with Barney as well, so much that in December 1860, he went to the political boss of New York City, Thurlow Weed, and told him he wanted to appoint Barney as the collector of customs for the Port of New York. This request from Lincoln created some political tension. Weed was a supporter of William H. Seward from New York during the Republican National Convention, but his candidate had lost the bid just as Chase did. Chase and Seward were political rivals, but Weed had little choice but to honor Lincoln's wish. Both Seward and Chase were also rivals of Lincoln, but he appointed Chase as secretary of the treasury and Seward as secretary of state nonetheless.

This created an interesting predicament for Barney. He had political enemies surrounding him, and his position as the collector of customs presented many opportunities for corruption. In his position, Barney supervised about 580 employees with a combined payroll of over $700,000. In addition, he was dealing with a large portion of the foreign commerce coming to and from the United States.

There was an incident of corruption under Barney's watch concerning Henry B. Stanton, one of his deputies, in 1863. Stanton was accused of accepting bribes to cancel bonds that were securities against an illicit shipment of goods. It turned out the person taking the bribes was Neil Stanton, Henry's son. It was swept under the rug, and Henry denied any wrongdoing. Later that same year, he left his position.

Hiram was trusted by Lincoln so much that on September 5, 1862, Lincoln met with Barney at the Navy Department. He took out a paper he had been working on, the Emancipation Proclamation, and asked Barney's opinion. Barney suggested a change to it, which Lincoln included. On September 22, just a couple of weeks later, Lincoln issued his preliminary version of the Emancipation Proclamation to the world.

The political games continued around Barney and challenged his loyalty to either Lincoln or Chase. Chase supported Barney, and Barney lent Chase $5,000, which secured that loyalty even more. In 1864, Chase ran against Lincoln as the Republican frontrunner for the presidency. Both Lincoln and Chase expected loyalty from Hiram Barney. Chase resigned as the secretary of the treasury in order to run. Barney was also asked to resign. Lincoln would need the vote of New York and did not feel he could get it if Barney remained in his position.

Barney chose to resign and went back to practicing law. Chase lost the nomination, and Lincoln went on to be reelected as president. Without bitter political feelings, Lincoln immediately nominated Chase as chief justice of the Supreme Court. Chase took the position and remained until his death.

LEWIS T. BARNEY

Lewis T. Barney, son of Hiram Barney, was born in 1844. During the Civil War, Lewis became the youngest brevet brigadier general in the entire Union army. He first enlisted in the Seventh New York State Militia on May 25, 1862, at the age of eighteen. He started as a first lieutenant in Company F and mustered out of the militia on September 5 that same year. Shortly after, he was commissioned in Company D of the Sixty-Eighth New York on November 20, 1862. He served with the company until February 29, 1864, at which point he was discharged for promotion and commissioned to the Adjutant General's Department of the United States Volunteers. Sometime during this period, he was listed as a captain, and he served on the staff of General Rufus Saxon as assistant adjutant general. On June 21, 1864, he resigned.

Lewis Barney was offered a commission as the colonel of the 106th New York but declined. Instead, he was granted the authority of the governor to recruit the 180th New York on May 24, 1864. He was not able to fulfill his task of recruiting a regiment, but he was able to recruit one company,

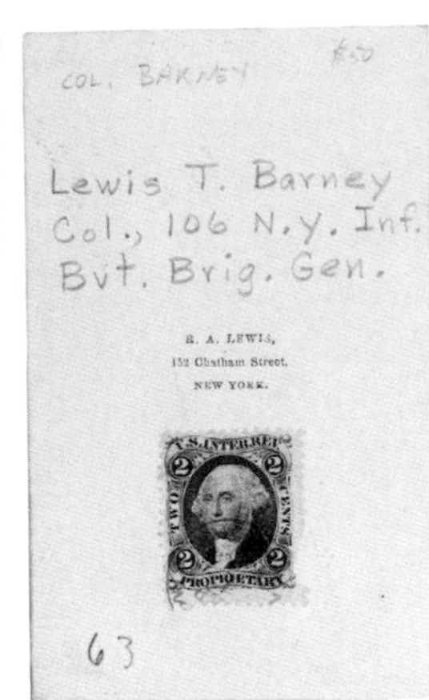

A carte de visite of Lewis T. Barney. R.A. Lewis was the photographer, and the photo was taken during the Civil War, when Barney was given the title of brigadier general. *Tom Gardner Collection.*

which was then sent to the 179th New York. Because of his failure, he was given a commission, and his authority to recruit a regiment was revoked in August 1864. He continued to serve and received brevets dated March 13, 1865, both as a brigadier and a major general of United States Volunteers, for "gallant and meritorious services during the war." This was less than a week before his twenty-first birthday. He had become the youngest brevet brigadier general in the Union army. This honor was not bestowed upon him for his outstanding achievements in his military career but more as a mechanism as an officer during the war.

Barney had been injured during combat, which resulted in total deafness in one ear and partial deafness in the other. Hiram Barney wanted to do something to help his veteran son, as his prospects could be limited due to his injury. Hiram recalled his dream years prior of building a vineyard in Keokuk, Iowa, and so he sent Lewis to the site to build and manage the White Elk Vineyard.

The city directories at the time list Lewis Barney as living in the area in the late 1860s, and his job was listed as major general. A few years later, the directories list him as the manager of White Elk Vineyard. His residence was listed as 630 Grand Avenue. It was built and still owned by his father, Hiram.

Lewis seemed to have a knack for growing grapes and making wine. Within the first ten years, he was producing upward of 30,000 gallons of wine. His wines were highly regarded and sought after and won medals at agricultural exhibitions. He built four underground domed limestone cellars eighteen by two hundred feet long, as well as an underground fermenting room. The cellars could hold over 100,000 gallons of wine. The vineyard produced wine from Catawba, Concord, Ives, Norton,

A drawing of the home of J.F. Daughtery, the owner of an alcohol distributor in Keokuk, Iowa, in the late 1890s. *Collection Michael White, ISU Extension and Outreach Viticulture Specialist.*

Delaware, Clinton, Iona and Alvey grapes. The wines were sold as far south as New Orleans and as far west as Denver. This placed winemaking in Iowa as a legitimate industry.

Hiram Barney was still the owner of the White Elk Vineyard, but he was getting up in years, so he decided to incorporate. The original officers were:

- The Honorable John H. Craig, president
- General Lewis T. Barney, vice president
- The Honorable Edward Jaeger, secretary and treasurer
- Mr. Buel Hambden, director
- Honorable Hiram Barney, director

During the period of incorporation, Hiram's wife, Susan, passed away. Susan was the daughter of the famous abolitionist Louis Tappen. Susan was not well before her death, and in 1864, Hiram wrote a letter to a friend in England saying she had been confined to a Philadelphia insane asylum.

Hiram Barney began courting Harriet Kilbourne, the granddaughter of his old friend David W. Kilbourne, sometime in the 1870s. In August 1880,

To Dealers who desire to furnish pure Wines to their trade, we wish to call their attention to the fact that they are acknowledged to be the finest produced in this country. We do not manufacture and palm them off for Wine, under a foreign label. These Wines have received the endorsement of many of the Leading Physicians and are daily prescribed by them to those who want something for a digester. They are fine Table Wines. If the trade will not handle them, they can be had direct from the Cellars by the Case, Keg or Barrel.

For Price List, or other information, address 1876.

WHITE ELK VINEYARDS,

KEOKUK, : : : : : : IOWA.

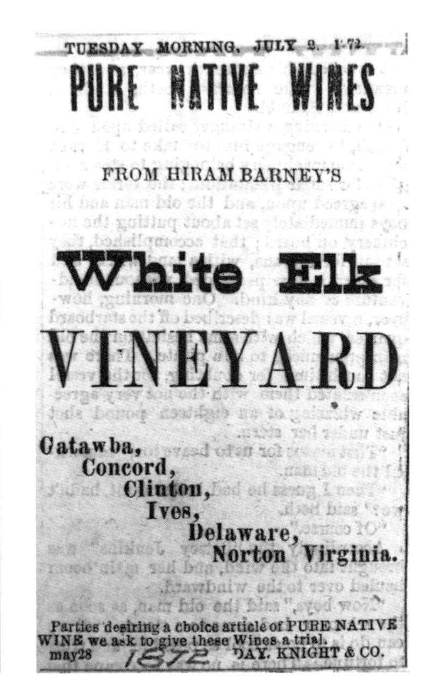

Left: Advertisement for White Elk Vineyards in Keokuk, Iowa, 1876. At the time, wine was thought to be a good tonic for digestion and was often doctor-endorsed to be drank daily. The advertisement was for wine dealers and distributors. *Daily Gate City*.

Right: An advertisement for White Elk wines in the *Gate City* paper in Keokuk. The varietals being made at the time are listed; most are native American vines. The cold-hardy hybrids used in most modern wineries were not created until the twentieth century. July 2, 1872. *Daily Gate City*.

"Fruit of the vine—as old as civilization itself, as it appeared in the White Elk Vineyard," Keokuk, Iowa, August 30, 1863. *Daily Gate City*.

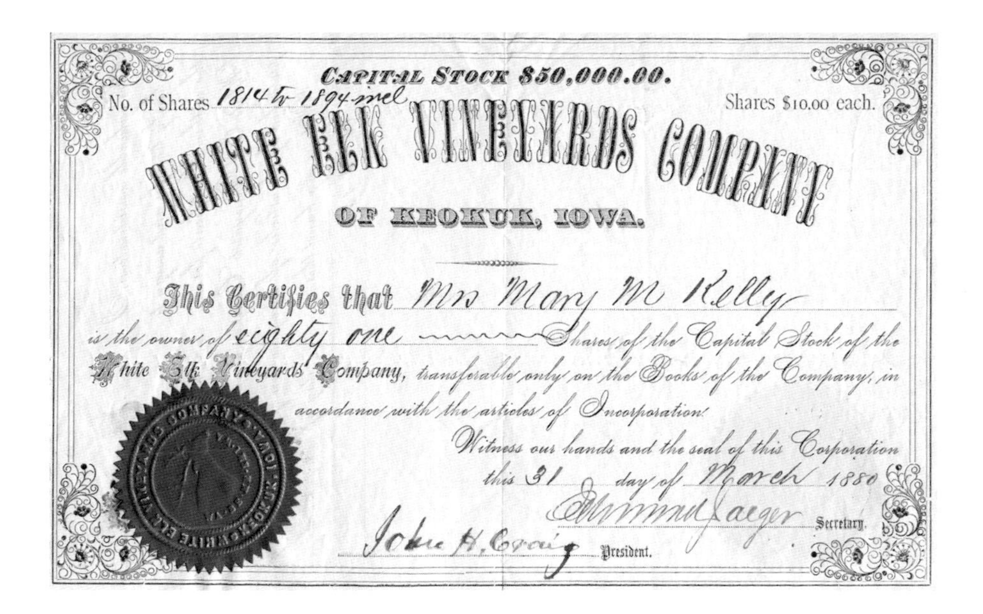
CAPITAL STOCK $50,000.00.
No. of Shares 1814 to 1894 incl Shares $10.00 each.
WHITE ELK VINEYARDS COMPANY
OF KEOKUK, IOWA.

This Certifies that Mrs Mary M Kelly
is the owner of eighty one Shares of the Capital Stock of the White Elk Vineyards Company, transferable only on the Books of the Company, in accordance with the articles of Incorporation.
Witness our hands and the seal of this Corporation this 31 day of March 1880

Jaeger Secretary.
John H. Craig President.

Above: A stock certificate for eighty-one shares owned by Mrs. Mary M. Kelly of the White Elk Vineyards, March 31, 1880. Shares were sold for $10 apiece for a total cost of $8,100, which was a significant amount of money in the late nineteenth century. *Tom Gardner Collection*.

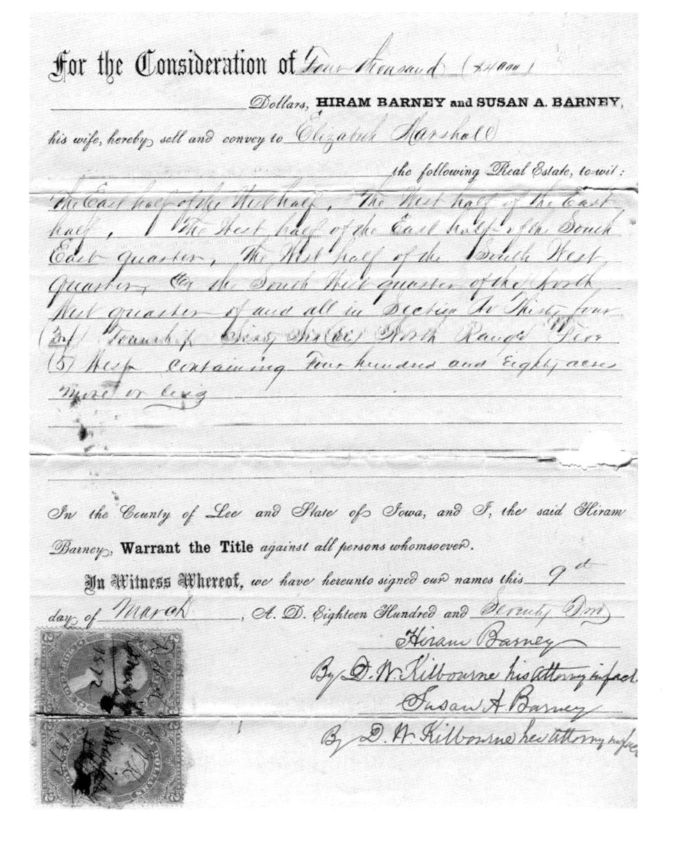
For the Consideration of Four thousand ($4000) Dollars, HIRAM BARNEY and SUSAN A. BARNEY, his wife, hereby sell and convey to Elizabeth Marshall the following Real Estate, to-wit: The East half of the West half, The West half of the East half, The West half of the East half of the South East quarter, The West half of the South West quarter, & the South West quarter of the North West quarter of and all in Section No Thirty four (34) Township Sixty Six (66) North Range Five (5) West containing Four hundred and Eighty acres more or less

In the County of Lee and State of Iowa, and I, the said Hiram Barney, Warrant the Title against all persons whomsoever.

In Witness Whereof, we have hereunto signed our names this 9th day of March, A. D. Eighteen Hundred and Seventy One

Hiram Barney
By D. W. Kilbourne his attorney in fact
Susan A Barney
By D. W. Kilbourne her attorney in fact

Right: A title signed by Hiram Barney for land attached to the White Elk Winery to be sold to Elizabeth Marshall. Barney sold off land he had acquired in Lee County. *Tom Gardner Collection*.

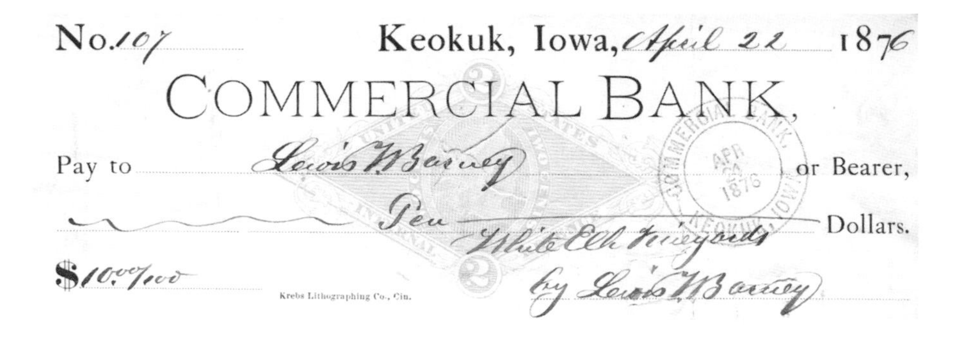

No. 107 Keokuk, Iowa, April 22 1876

COMMERCIAL BANK.

Pay to Lewis T. Barney or Bearer,

Ten Dollars.

$10 00/100

Krebs Lithographing Co., Cin.

White Elk Vineyard

by Lewis T. Barney

Above: A check signed by Lewis T. Barney on behalf of the White Elk Vineyard, April 22, 1876, in the amount of ten dollars. *Tom Gardner Collection*.

Right: Lewis T. Barney in a photograph taken some years after the war ended. It seems likely that it was taken while he was running the White Elk Vineyard, but he may have been back in New York for a GAR reunion. Photographer unknown. Barney was the youngest man to be brevetted to brigadier general and major general during the war. *Tom Gardner Collection*.

the two decided to have a May-December marriage; Harriet was twenty-two and Hiram was sixty-nine. Hiram had six children with his first wife, Susan, and two additional children with Harriet. On May 18, 1895, Hiram passed away in Spuyten Duyvil, in the Bronx, at the age of eighty-four.

At some point—the exact time is hard to determine—Lewis T. Barney stopped running the White Elk Vineyard. His tragic death occurred on December 19, 1904. He was living in Los Angeles, California, with his wife. He was walking down a street while reading a newspaper. Because he was deaf, he could not hear the horse-drawn wagon that ran him over.

CHESTER P. CORY

There were changes around the township of Keokuk, notably the construction of the Des Moines Rapids Canal. This was a stretch of twelve miles of rapids that were not far from the White Elk Vineyard. The rapids were dangerous at high water, and at low water, they were rocky and impassable. During these times, cargo had to be unloaded from boats and carried past the rapids in a horse-drawn wagon.

Lieutenant Robert E. Lee headed a project from 1831 to 1833 to blast the largest rocks in the rapids and remove some of the debris that made passage impossible. While this did make the rapids marginally safer during high water, it did not solve the problem. Lee recommended a canal be built to solve the issue, but his vision would have to wait until after the Civil War.

Actual construction began in 1866. The canal started at Keokuk stretched eight miles and provided a channel around the rapids. It opened in 1877. Four more miles of canal were built south of Keokuk and extended to the Des Moines River. The depth of the canal was only five feet. Over time, boats increased in size and could no longer make it through the canal. The government responded by building a large dam, a power plant and a new

A view of the old canal as seen from the Cory home and yard at White Elk Vineyards, reproduced from picture of that day owned by Chester Cory. *Daily Gate City.*

Left: Mr. and Mrs. Hugh Cory pictured at their home in Mount Sterling, Illinois. Hugh Cory was the son of Chester Cory, who owned the White Elk Winery from 1903 to 1914. *Daily Gate City*.

Below: Typical wine cellar entrance at the White Elk Winery. They were underground to keep the wine cool. The ruins of these arches still exist today. *Daily Gate City*.

A street sign in Keokuk for Old Vineyard Road, which marks the area where White Elk Vineyard once stood. *Collection Michael White, ISU Extension and Outreach Viticulture Specialist.*

White Elk Vineyard ruins in Keokuk. Rocks have obscured the entrances of what were once the winery's wine cellars. White Elk at its zenith produced fifteen thousand to thirty thousand gallons a year. *Collection Michael White, ISU Extension and Outreach Viticulture Specialist.*

Top: A top view of the collapsed wine cellar at White Elk Winery, 2018. These ruins were recently discovered and are located one and a half miles north of Keokuk. *Collection Michael White, ISU Extension and Outreach Viticulture Specialist.*

Bottom: Remnants of glass wine bottles and metal bands used in wine barrel cooperage discovered around the ruins of the White Elk Vineyard, February 2018. *Collection Michael White, ISU Extension and Outreach Viticulture Specialist.*

A vent to the wine cellar below at the ruins of the White Elk Vineyard. Venting is necessary to allow heat to escape and keep the wine cool. *Collection Michael White, ISU Extension and Outreach Viticulture Specialist.*

Panama-sized lock system. This created a six-foot navigation channel. In 1913, the canal was closed and the new channel opened; it is used to this day.

Chester P. Cory purchased the White Elk Vineyard in 1903. He kept it open until the opening of the new dam.

Chester was a teetotaler, and instead of producing wine, he produced grape juice. He did sell juice to a local patent medicine firm that made an "elixir of life" with it. Before closing the vineyard, Cory refused to sell any land to the firm building the dam until it agreed to build a river road from Keokuk to Montrose above the dam's reservoir.

There is still some evidence of the massive cellars that existed beneath the White Elk Vineyard.

Chapter 4

COUNCIL BLUFFS GRAPE GROWERS ASSOCIATION

While the Barneys were building White Elk Vineyard, there was a lot of activity in western Iowa, in Council Bluffs. Grapes were grown in Council Bluffs as early as 1857. It began when A.S. Bonham settled near Council Bluffs and set out a vineyard on the hills about one and a half miles from the courthouse. He was able to sell his grapes for as much as one dollar for a ten-pound basket of grapes. In a report of grape production and distribution in western Iowa, the following was remarked upon:

> *Agricultural Experiment Station—Iowa State College of Agriculture and Mechanic Arts*
>
> *Grape growing as a commercial proposition in western Iowa, started in the vicinity of Council Bluffs as early as 1857. The Council Bluffs district has about 500 acres of bearing vines and 200 acres on non-bearing age, or a total of about 700 acres.*

Commercial grape growing was unusually successful in Council Bluffs because the area was naturally adapted to the industry.

The wine-growing industry began taking off a few years later. In the *Report of the Iowa State Horticultural Society* for 1886, it was noted:

> *Grapes—The crop of this fruit was very heavy, and of course the Concord was the variety that predominated, though Worden is considerable planted of late, and the fruit has appeared in the markets. This fruit is produced*

in the river counties in such quantities that the price is very low, so that even "poor people" can indulge in a basket of grapes occasionally. The Concord in at about seven cents per pound and were down as low as two and one half cents towards the close of the season. I have been told that Worden rated on to two cents higher than Concord as long as the crop lasted. Moore's Early is an attractive variety, on account of the large size of the berries. The fruit of this variety sold at eight cents per pound, chiefly from the fact that it comes into market about four weeks before the Concord. The fruit of this variety is possibly a little better than Concord, but its chief value consists in its earliness. It is estimated that in the city of Council Bluffs alone there was five hundred baskets of grapes handled every day during the grape season, and nearly double that amount in Omaha. A large portion of those grapes handled in Omaha are grown in the border counties of Iowa. This should indicate that the grape business in the Third District is simply immense. Some of the newer varieties, such as Niagara, Empire State, Cottage, etc., grow here luxuriantly, but we fear they will need some protection in the northern part of our district. Probably in the southern tier of counties, on the Missouri line, they will be perfectly hardy.

The Council Bluffs Grape Growers Association was very instrumental in the success of grape growing in western Iowa. It provided markets for grapes at the best possible prices to growers and, in addition, low-cost marketing. This meant that grape growing was more organized and more successful than in other parts of Iowa. On June 30, 1891, the *Omaha Daily Bee* reported on the Council Bluffs Grape Growers Association. The cooperative organization was a significant force in the growth of the wine industry in Iowa through Prohibition. The *Bee* noted, "The headquarters of the Council Bluffs Grape Growers association at 201 Broadway was the sight [*sic*] of great activity, for the association was handling all the output, and shipping direct to customers the same day the fruit was picked. The supply was great, and the orders promptly filled."

The Iowa State Horticultural Society discussed the marketing of grapes through the Council Bluffs Grape Growers Association. Its influence began growing, and so did the demand for grapes and wine. The concept of the association was that a cooperative group of winemakers with similar goals would work together. The association could market stronger together than individually.

The following was included in the *Report of the Iowa State Horticultural Society for the Year 1893*:

Marketing the Grape by J.P. Hess, Council Bluffs
In extending our vineyards we must look around for a market for our products. Select a location that has advantages regarding transportation facilities as well as a good home market.

These are matters of the greatest importance to the grape grower. After a market has been well established it is important that our products should be brought to the consumer with the least possible expense. And there is no way in which that can be accomplished better than by the growers uniting and organizing an association for the handling of their products.

A well-managed organization has a great advantage over the commission house by concentrating the business that otherwise would be divided among a number of rival commission firms, who, being eager to get the business, often make a sacrifice of the product without considering the interest of the grower.

Such has been our experience in by-gone days before the advent of our association. Grapes brought to the commission house, one day brought twenty cents a basket; from what was delivered the next day, of the same kind and quality, the returns were only ten cents a basket and even less.

But the Council Bluffs Grape Growers' Shipping Association we have a new departure, a market that varies a shade from day to day, of course. But as the consumption of this fruit for different purposes increase, there is no reason we cannot sell our grapes the same as we sell our corn and hogs.

To consign at random to the commercial cities within our territory can only result in loss and confusion to the grower.

The Council Bluffs Grape Growers Association was formed in 1892, but after a year, its members were already seeing the results of their cooperative effort. At the time it began, the vineyard area of the district was only about one hundred acres. Hess's essay continues:

Our association, which is less than a year old, has given us satisfactory results, and it is no longer a question with us whether we can establish a market for our grapes at home, and do not have to send them five hundred or one thousand miles away from home, asking someone to give us a bid. Better dump them in vats and make wine and vinegar than follow a system that is so certain of ruinous results to the grower. The past season we shipped about thirty-three car loads of grapes through the association, and every basket was sold before it left Council Bluffs.

Because the group could produce grapes and have them processed cooperatively, it was able to lower the price of the grapes. Members could share resources and equipment. Their main objective was selling the grapes, not necessarily making wine with them. This did not occur until later after the turn of the century.

Hess continued:

> *Grapes can be produced so cheaply that every family can afford to use them. They are a staple and a necessity, as much as the potato therefore, they should have a fixed value, regulated only by the supply and demand. Now, when we have established the fact that we will gain by a combination for handling our crop, we will have the best results by observing strict business methods and taking the greatest care in packing and grading, so that buyers will know what they buy. We are now using nine-pound grape baskets, which seem to give general satisfaction, both to grower and dealer.*
>
> *With good, ripe fruit, carefully packed and thoroughly inspected, success is assured for marketing grapes by the association method, both as to economy and by stimulating and developing the industry.*

Not only could they share in production resources, but association members could also benefit from marketing and shipping resources as well. In 1893, the association's president, M.J. Williams, reported:

> *Council Bluffs has a fruit shippers' association that has been a great benefit to its members. There is a membership fee of $10.00, which entitles the members to a share of the stock of the association. We have forty odd members, making the capital stock over $400. The affairs of the association are managed by a board of directors. We did not pay them for their time this year, but we propose to pay them in the future. The manager is the principal man, and conducts the business. He is hired by the board and gets $125 per month for about five months. It requires a thorough business man to conduct the business successfully. He has not sent out grapes on commission, but send out price lists, and sells, mostly by the car load. Most of our grapes went to Sioux City, Minneapolis, Denver, Kansas City and Chicago.*

In the book *A History of Wine in America: From the Beginnings to Prohibition*, Thomas Pinney writes about some of the driving forces of grape growing in western Iowa and eastern Nebraska:

> *A report on his operations in 1896 noted that Pitz's success had stimulated "a number of German capitalists" to investigate the chances of winegrowing in Nebraska. No extensive development followed, but a small industry has persisted in the region, especially on the opposite bank of the Missouri, in Iowa, around Council Bluffs....*
>
> *...Meanwhile, a series of bitter schisms among the Icarians, culminating in the exile and death of their leader, Etienne Cabet, had left the Nauvoo community weak and disorganized. In the hope of making a new start, some Icarians migrated to the southwestern corner of Iowa in 1860, not far from that stretch of the Missouri River where the borders of Iowa, Nebraska, Kansas, and Missouri approach one another between Omaha and Kansas City. Here they established a small vineyard of Concord vines expressly for winemaking and succeeded in maintaining it for many years. Even after another schism had sent the last expedition of Icarians out to California, the Icarians who remained in Iowa kept their vineyard going. The example had some effect, for as early as 1870 nearby Des Moines County had 250 acres in vines and was producing 30,000 gallons of wine from standard American varieties. It was reported in 1898 that the example of the Icarians had made grape growing a success in southwestern Iowa.*

The Council Bluffs Grape Growers Association held a meeting on August 8, 1898, at which members suggested participating in a "Grape Day." They extended their invitation to all the fruit growers to create a display that would be "a credit to Pottawattamie county." The members of the association would be on hand to provide samples of their large yield of grapes that year. They wanted visitors to see and taste the quality of grapes the county could produce.

The association continued to grow, and each year it produced and shipped more grapes to the East than in previous years. Most of the grapes being grown were Concord grapes, which accounted for more than 90 percent of the crops. In addition, there were Worden, Moore Early and Niagara grapes grown. The Moore Early grapes only composed a small percentage of the market and were sold in four-pound baskets. Only about four thousand baskets of the varietal were sold in an average season.

The Niagara grapes were only grown in small quantities because the demand for white grapes was low. They did not sell well in local markets, and when sent with shipments of black grapes, they would often be rejected or the price of the black grape baskets would be reduced.

Worden grapes were also a smaller crop, but they were at times mixed in with Concord vineyards, and often they were considered the same as Concord grapes. The Worden grapes would ripen a few days ahead of the Concord grapes. They did not ship as well as the Concord grapes, and they would often crack.

FACTORS FOR THE ASSOCIATION TO CONSIDER

One of the advantages that the Council Bluffs Grape Growers Association offered was its transportation facilities. There were some factors for the association to consider and work through, such as geographic location, ripening season, yield of competing grape districts, competition with other varieties of fruit and fixed charges of transportation.

Council Bluffs had nine main railroads that passed through its city, and the connections reached from the Mississippi River to the Rocky Mountains. There were six lines that covered the territories east toward Chicago. There were three others that went from Kansas City and St. Louis. Two connections extended southwest into the Kansas and Oklahoma territories. Still three others covered the region west to Denver and to the Rocky Mountains. Three connections extended northwest into the Dakotas and Montana. And four more covered the area into the Minnesota territory. These rails allowed over two hundred freight trains to leave from the Council Bluffs area, which allowed the grape growers in the region to unload their harvests quickly to a wide distribution network.

Because of their geographic location, Council Bluffs grape growers had an advantage over their competitors and traded heavily in the Great Plains area. They were close to market, which also reduced the costs of shipping grapes. And because of their location, their grapes ripened sooner than many of their competitors along the Missouri River.

Council Bluffs did not have too much competition from other varieties of fruit. For instance, Colorado purchased many grapes even though its peach season was at its height in the same region at the same time.

Because the association was able to collectively bargain, members were able to get the best fixed rates for transportation costs. Because of these factors, they were leaders in selling grapes not only in Iowa but in all the Midwest territories.

WINTER CHALLENGE

There were challenges specific to the Midwest, and bad winter weather was a major one. Bad weather devastated the wine industry in 1889. The Iowa State Horticultural Society said the following in its 1901 report:

> *Before the severe winter of 1889 we would point with pride at our success in grape culture in Western Iowa and would frequently compare it with our corn crop. In fact, we went farther: we would boast of our grape crop being more sure of producing a profitable crop than our cornfields. We were justified in making these claims, as the oldest vineyards had never failed to produce profitable crops up to that time. The destruction of fully half of our vines and weakening the balance to such an extent that it was questioned whether we could recuperate them to such an extent as to be considered of any value....*
>
> *...I have received the figures from the manager of the Council Bluffs Grape Growers' Shipping Association showing the amount of grapes shipped from Council Bluffs for the years 1901, 1900, 1899, 1898 and 1897, which was the banner year for the Council Bluffs Grape-Growers. 1897, 102 cars; 1898, 50 cars; 1899, 8 cars; 1900, 20 cars and 1901, 37 cars.*
>
> *We learn from the above figures that we are gradually creeping up to our former prosperity, but we will take some time to regain the ground we have lost, but the experience we have gained, though costly, was not any the less valuable. We have discovered that not all soils and locations can be depended upon when these test winters come, and we shall select for our vineyards only choicest locations, south or southeast slopes. I had a vineyard, part a southeast slope and part a southwest slope nearly all lived and are bearing good grapes again.*
>
> *We should take pains to plant our plants as deep as it is possible for us to plant them, and plant only the strongest and most thrifty plants.*
>
> *The outlook is encouraging. There is no other fruit that promises better and surer returns than the grape. Our markets are assured. We have a territory that can expect to supply with grapes for years to come. The country north and south of us will be only able to raise them in limited quantities, if at all, and they will look to us for their supply of grapes. Unless the unexpected happens, we will in a few more years return to our former prosperity in grape culture.*

Farmers during the early twentieth century did not have the technology and understanding of hybridization that we do today. They struggled with breeding plants that, although cold-hardy, could not endure severe weather conditions. The industry continued to struggle but had not given up quite yet in western Iowa.

Homer Field and the Honorable Joseph Reed wrote in *History of Pottawattamie County*:

> *Fruit raising during the early settlement of the county was not attended with much success. At first the young trees would kill out during the winters, some of which were severe, but the real cause was found to be the long distance from which they were brought.*
>
> *A few of the pioneers, however, had faith, notably Mr. Terry, of Crescent; Mr. McDonald, of Kane; Mr. Cooledge, of Mills, and later, Mr. Raymond, of Garner, also Mr. Rice of Kane. Nurseries were started and fruit raising became infectious until at this time a farm without an orchard or vineyard, or both, is the exception. In a few years the crop more than supplied the home market, and steps were taken to find others.*
>
> *In 1891 a number of the fruit growers incorporated for mutual benefit with a capital of $1,000. A building was rented temporarily in which to handle the crop and they began shipping. The business grew and in 1905 the company elected a warehouse 36x60 feet of two stories and basement, in which the business was conducted for two years.*
>
> *In the spring of 1907 the company was reincorporated with a capital stock of $35,000 under the name of the Grape Growers' Association, with J.A. Aulabaugh, president; Alex. Wood, vice-president and chairman of the board of directors; J.J. Hess, secretary, and Charles Konigmacher, treasurer. The warehouse built, not being sufficient, an additional one has been added, 60x160 feet. This also is of brick, two stories and basement. The shipping facilities are of the best, being located on the Great Western track. The company has reliable agents in Minneapolis, St. Paul, Denver, Pueblo, Duluth and Salt Lake, besides intermediate points.*
>
> *The new warehouse above mentioned is probably the strongest in the city. It is already rented, to take effect as soon as the grape season closes, for storage of 150 carloads or 7,500,000 pounds of sugar.*
>
> *Among the leading fruit growers of western Pottawattamie are Rev. G.G. Rice, D.L. Royer, Robert McKinsey, A. Wood, D.J. Smith, W.T. Keeline, Harry Kingston, O.J. Smith, W.H. Kuhn, Mark L. Stageman, Chas. Konigmacher, Wm. Arnd, A. Rosner, J.W. Dorland, W.G. Rich, N.P.*

Dodge, Wm. Homburg, Anton Kerston, James Peterson, J.A. Alabaugh, T.F. Gretzer, C.D. Parmale, John Johnson, M.R. Smith, Henry Sperling, G.C. Hansen, Peter Peterson, Miss Nance Avery, Dr. A.P. Hanchett, J.F. Wilcox and Charles Beno.

In a 1909 issue of the *Fruit Grower*, the efforts of the Council Bluffs Grape Growers Association were mentioned:

If there is any one fruit which has been neglected in the Middle west of recent years it has been the grape....In certain sections grapes are extensively grown, as at Hermann, Mo., where they are grown for wine, and at Council Bluffs, Iowa where the fruit is sold fresh....

We stated that enough grapes should be planted in one locality to afford carlot shipments. For the encouragement of those who are interested we want to present some figures regarding the work of the Council Bluffs (Iowa) Grape Growers' Association, this information having been furnished by Mr. W.S. Keeline, who has been a leading worker in the association. Mr. Keeline says:

"Before the organization of the Council Bluffs Grape Growers' Association a number of growers were unable to dispose of all their fruit on the local markets, and when we attempted to consign to commission men in distant cities we found returns were not satisfactory. One car shipped to Sioux City, for instance, did not return a cent. According, we perfected our organization on December 24th, 1892. For fifteen years Mr. George Allingham was manager of the association, and when he died in 1907 he was succeeded by Mr. George Reye, who is still manager. Our association is a stock company, each member being a holder of one share of stock, at $10 a share, and every member is compelled to market all his fruits through the association. If he does not, he loses the dividends or accumulations of the association from that year's business.

"As the fruit is delivered to the association each day part is sold on the local market, part is sold in Omaha, and the remainder—which is by far the larger part—is shipped out. Every day's receipts are pooled at noon, so that the grower who delivers fruit today gets the average price of all that kind of fruit sold today. This is absolutely necessary, for our shipping orders usually bring the best price, and yet someone's stuff must be sold here at home and in Omaha.

"Our grapes are sold on track here, and our small fruits are shipped out to responsible dealers, mostly on standing orders, but all fruit is sold,

> *and never consigned. Our manger buys our box material, baskets, wire for trellises, posts and commercial fertilizer in carload lots and all is sold to the members at just enough of an advance to pay for the handling. At the end of the season the profits or such part of them as the directors may set aside for dividends, are divided among the members, each one's dividend being based on the quantity of fruit sold through the association.*
>
> *"We have two large brink warehouse buildings on trackage, which cost in the neighborhood of $40,000. In the fruit season these buildings are used to handle our crops, and in the winter one of these buildings is used to store sugar of the sugar trust. This sugar is stored here in transit. Our association has been successful, and we have just signed a contract under which for the coming season we will handle the crop of the Omaha Fruit-Growers' Association, our association acting as sales agent."*

In 1893, which was the first year the association was in business, it had a total volume of 94,814 baskets of grapes that sold for 19¼ cents per basket for a total value of $25,264.55. This volume remained constant until 1903, when the value amount reached $34,262.16. Then in 1905, it nearly doubled to $66,036.02, and by 1906, it had reached $89,009.37. The association decided to build a new warehouse, and its volume went to $120,669.11.

In 1907, Niagara grapes sold for $0.13½ per eight-pound basket and black grapes for $0.23½ per eight-pound basket and $0.22 per four-pound basket. But once again, the wine industry in western Iowa took a beating from the winter weather in 1908. There was a late freeze and a hailstorm that battered the vines. Other territories that grew grapes had good crops, and the eastern grape crop was unusually early and came in direct competition with the western fruit. This drove down the prices of the western Iowa grapes. Black grapes dropped to $0.18½ for an eight-pound basket and $0.21 for a four-pound basket.

It should be noted that transportation and the quality of grapes in the different-sized baskets affected pricing. Eight-pound baskets were standard to ship on trains to be processed. Because of the weight of the grapes, the ones on the bottom were crushed. The eight-pound baskets of grapes were used for juice and wine and were often shipped by rail. The four-pound baskets of grapes did not crush as easily and fetched a higher price. At different times, different-sized baskets were in higher demand, and therefore, the price fluctuated. You can still buy produce in bulk cheaper than those in small cartons in the supermarket. Grapes and other fruits are shipped and processed differently now, and many wineries process their grapes at their facilities or ones close to them rather than shipping them long distances.

W.S. Keeline said this in 1909 about the varying wine market:

> *There is much encouragement in this report, for it shows that when growers are properly organized returns are satisfactory. As a result of the work of the Council Bluffs Grape Grower's Association the growers are all in good spirits, and a constantly increasing acreage is being planted. Land values have risen until the Missouri River hill land is perhaps higher in price in the vicinity of Council Bluffs than in the neighborhood of any other town along the Missouri River—and yet there are thousands of acres from St. Louis to Council Bluffs which will grow just as good grapes, and the crop can be marketed just as profitably.*

Keeline must have been correct in his assessment because in 1909, the production of grapes was 11,708,330 pounds, valued at $330,078. The value of grapevines of bearing age in 1910 was $1,983,465; those not of bearing age was $446,126. The Council Bluffs Grape Growers Association was back on track for growth. Farmers were growing different varieties of grapes. Concord, Moore Early and Worden composed 90 percent of the planting, with the Concord proving most reliable and Moore Early generally most profitable per acre.

Keeline was a pioneer in the Iowa grape growing industry and helped with getting the association off the ground. His son Clarence Keeline was a grape grower of one hundred acres and was at one time the largest producer in the area. He was able to gain about $200 to $400 of profit per acre. In the 1920s, Clarence had transients help harvest the crops, as he needed about one hundred people to pick grapes during the harvest season. There would be camps of tents full of nomadic people who would arrive, pick the fruit and then move elsewhere for work. The workers consisted of men, women and children. The grapes were loaded on wide-runnered sleds and then pulled to the packinghouses, where they were weighed, inspected and placed on refrigerator cars for transport.

Keeline felt that the work and quality of fruit produced was largely taken for granted by the locals.

> *We yield the palm to no district when it comes to growing grapes economically and marketing them advantageously. People rave about California grapes but instead they should realize that we have better*

GRAPES ARE POPULAR CROP FOR WESTERN IOWA HILLS

One of the largest plots in the 100-acre vineyard on the Keeline fruit farm near Council Bluffs is seen in the picture below. The Keelines own the largest vineyard in western Iowa and probably the largest in Iowa. At the left above is the warehouse and office building of the Council Bluffs Grape Growers association, one of the pioneer fruit marketing organizations of the United States. Employes are busy now making 700,000 baskets to be used by the 125 members to market their mammoth grape crop this year. At the right above are the beauty contest winners at the recent Delaware county farm bureau, left to right, Lucile Logan, Lena Helmrich and Leola Johnston, first, second and third respectively.

One of the largest plots in the one-hundred-acre vineyard on the Keeline fruit farm near Council Bluffs. The Keelines owned the largest vineyard in western Iowa. On the left was the building that housed the Council Bluffs Grape Growers Association. On the right are the beauty contest winners of the Delaware County Farm Bureau. *From left to right*: Lucile Logan, Lena Helmrich and Leola Johnston. August 8, 1926. *Des Moines Register.*

Resourceful Mormons in 1856 planted grapes on the hills of Council Bluffs as they stopped by the Missouri River on their way west. This is the Harry Martin vineyard, east of Council Bluffs. These are Concord grapes, which were commonly planted in Iowa. September 19, 1943. *Des Moines Register.*

Little Sylvia Rasmussen, who lived on a big farm near Council Bluffs where there were many grapes, is helping in the harvest. All the older boys and girls worked in the vineyards. *Des Moines Register.*

grape growing conditions than does the far western state. We should have thousands of acres of grapes instead of hundreds. Grapes can be grown so successfully in but few spots in the world and nothing that farmers grow here pays nearly as well as grapes.

Because the association concentrated on growing and shipping grapes abroad rather than focusing on making wine, it continued to prosper during Prohibition. By 1920, the vineyards had expanded to about five hundred acres of bearing vines and about two hundred acres of younger vines. A 1921 report of "Grape Production and Distribution in Western Iowa" by the Agricultural Experiment Station–Iowa State College of Agriculture and Mechanic Arts included the following information about the Council Bluffs Grape Growers Association:

- The Council Bluffs district has about seven hundred acres of grapevines.
- The natural advantages that this district enjoys with respect to climate, soil and freedom from insects and disease make it a grape region of unlimited possibilities.
- The Concord grape composes over 90 percent of the vineyard acreage.
- The acre cost of production in a commercial vineyard is estimated at $143.75 and the gross receipts at $261.40. The profits, based on these estimates, from an acre of vineyard are $117.25.
- Vineyard management practice has not kept pace with the marketing organization. Closer attention on the part of growers to the improvement of cultural practices should result in higher and more economical production.
- The average acre yield varies, according to the size of the vineyard, from about 612 six-pound baskets in smaller vineyards to from 986 to 1,000 baskets in the larger acreages. The small growers are not securing maximum yields and should more closely follow the management practices of the larger vineyardist.
- The Council Bluffs district has an unusually favorable location as regards transportation facilities and accessibility to a large consuming territory.

- A total of 90 percent of the district production is marketed in carload quantities.
- The method of selling all grapes f.o.b. Council Bluffs relieves the grower of all risk of a change in the demands of the consuming market while a car is en route.
- Carlot wholesalers estimate an average of 100 to 150 baskets of grapes are unfit for sale on arrival at far distance points. This loss is due largely to the crushing of the baskets because of the weight above and shifting of the load and may be prevented by proper loading.
- An earlier ripening season, together with the percentage of an average crop in either the Wathena or Nauvoo district, influences to a considerable extent the destination of carload shipments of grapes from Council Bluffs from year to year.
- No grapes are shipped southwest from Council Bluffs, and only a relatively few cars go east into Iowa. This is probably due to shipments from the Nauvoo district and also to the fact that the western district has developed a demand for the Iowa grapes.
- In disposing of the present production of grapes from this region, there seems to be no very serious competition with other varieties of fruit.
- Railroad mileage is not as important in the shipping of grapes as is the attention or lack of attention given to the loading, routing and icing of the car while in route.
- The Council Bluffs Grape Growers Association is a very efficient sales agency. It handles about 89 percent of the total production of the district. The selling cost to its members has averaged only 6.1 percent during the past ten years.
- The commission firms probably offer a desirable outlet of marketing for growers who desire to pack their fruit above the average or in an extra fancy way. The daily pooling method of the association permits no premium for those who pack their fruit above the standard of the association requirements. However, only a very few growers pack their grapes enough above the association requirements to entitle them to a premium in price.
- During the years 1912–22, the date of the first grape picking has varied from August 3 in 1914 to August 29 in 1915. The closing dates have varied from September 21 in 1914 to October 14 in 1913.

The Council Bluffs Grape Growers Association did not fear competition from California. Henry Martin, the manager of the association for nearly three decades, said:

> *We usually can put our grapes on the market here in the middle west as cheaply as can California or any other growing area. We usually do not have to sacrifice in order to dispose of our crop, however. We are helped by the fact that our grapes ripen at a time when there are no others being marketed. There are small areas at Montrose, Ia. and Nauvoo, Ill., which compete with us, but we are able to seek markets that are more advantageous to us and the western Iowa grape growers receive more for their product than the members of any other cooperative organization in the United States.*

In 1931, the council began making grape juice instead of just shipping grapes. The Great Depression brought grapes from thirty-seven to forty cents per five-pound basket to ten cents per basket. Harry Martin said in an interview with the *Des Moines Register* on September 19, 1943, "When we sold grapes they had to be sold and eaten in 30 days. People just couldn't eat up that many in so short a time. So we started making grape juice—which can be sold the year around, at times when the market is good." The council pressed out and pasteurized the juice into gallon jugs and stored them. After aging the juice for three months, it was rebottled in pint and quart bottles to be sold in market.

In August 1940, there was a photo of the Grape Growers Association in the *Des Moines Register* that read, "Workmen at the Council Bluffs Grape Growers Association winery move one of the 18 vats recently purchased. Fifteen of the vats are being moved into the basement of the new addition to the association….Each vat holds 3,500 gallons of wine."

The Council Bluffs Grape Growers Association was in the winemaking business. The association was set up like other cooperative creameries and grain elevators at the time. Each member of the association held an equal vote. They could receive their pay upon the delivery of their grapes. Each season, the profits of the cooperative were figured and paid out according to the pounds delivered.

Betty Ann was the association's flagship wine. An advertisement from the *Spencer Daily Reporter* for Betty Ann Port Wine boasted the following:

> *For that Final Festive Touch—Betty Ann Port Wine!*
> *You're the perfect host when you serve your friends a sparkling glass of Betty Ann Port—at dessert time…cocktail…anytime. Rich and ruby with*

Above: Phyllis Torrell was one of the workers at a plant with grapes and the juice products that have brought Council Bluffs renown. Behind her is a stack of residue left after the juice was squeezed out. Farmers used the waste for hog feed and vineyard fertilizer. September 19, 1953. *Des Moines Register.*

Left: After it was pasteurized, grape juice was bottled in gallon jugs at the Council Bluffs cooperative plant. The juice aged for three months and then was rebottled in pint and quart bottles. Irene Wahl is pictured operating the machine. *Des Moines Register.*

luscious flavor of ripe Concord grapes, Betty Ann Port Wine is as sociable as mistletoe...as welcome as Santa Claus. Buy several bottles today, and be prepared when Holiday guests drop in. Try Betty Ann White Port, Muscatel, Tokay and Sherry.

Made from the fruit of the world's finest vineyards. Adds magic to cooking, glamour to desserts, smartness to entertaining. Yet, costs only a few cents a serving.

Available at any Iowa State Liquor Store

WAR ENDS WINEMAKING

During World War II, the War Food Administration (WFA) made decisions about how the nation's agricultural products would be handled. It ordered that no more wine was to be manufactured and that grapes needed to be pressed into juice or sold on the market. The Council Bluffs Grape Growers Association had to switch from winemaking to grape juice once again. The price for grape juice was not as good as it was for wine, so profits plummeted.

The association had to sell off the 80,000 to 100,000 gallons of wine it had produced and had aging in its cellars. Some of the wine was still young and not fully matured. Most of the wine had been sold through Iowa State liquor stores, but the majority of the juice was marketed in Nebraska. In 1943, the juice was being sold under the label "Blue Bird" for thirty to thirty-five cents a quart.

AFTER THE WAR

By 1947, the association was back to making wine along with juice pressing. The group improved its facilities and purchased $100,000 worth of new machinery. This included a new bottling line that allowed workers to produce 800 bottles a day rather than 250.

The council also produced wines from California grapes in addition to ones created from Iowa native wines, sometimes blending the two. It began producing 100,000 gallons of wine and 60,000 gallons of grape juice and employed thirty workers. In 1947, grape farmers harvested about

Doris Evans operating new bottling equipment at the cooperative Council Bluffs Grape Growers Association plant, October 26, 1947. *Des Moines Register.*

one million pounds of grapes at a rate of $120 a ton. This was double the rate from 1942.

The success of the wine industry in Council Bluffs continued for some years, but there were factors that eventually devastated not only the Council Bluffs area but grape growing in the entire state.

Chapter 5

AMANA COLONIES

TEN WINERIES

European homesteaders in Iowa established small vineyards on their farms to supply fresh grapes and to make juice, wine and jam at home for their families. The Amana Colonies were one such community. Amana was founded in 1714 by a sect called the Inspirationists, a piestic religious movement from Himbach, Germany. They were driven out of Germany because of their refusal to bear arms, send their children to school or conform with other civic duties. The Inspirationists were persecuted and congregated on estates in the German province of Hessen. In his book *A History of Wine in America: From the Beginnings to Prohibition*, Thomas Pinney says this about the Amana Colonies:

> *As for winemaking in religious communities, that, too, was represented in the Midwest, at least in a token way, in the Amana Colonies in southeastern Iowa, still flourishing 130 years after their founding by the German Community True Inspiration in 1854. On 25,000 acres of splendid Iowa soil, the Inspirationalists* [sic] *quietly developed a prosperous economy based on farming, cabinetmaking, meat smoking, and winemaking, carried out in seven small villages scattered over an area of some twenty square miles. Like the houses of the Rappites in Economy, Pennsylvania, those in the Amanas, often brick-built, had their walls covered with trellises for the growing of grapes. Winemaking was largely for local consumption; in the communal scheme of distribution, the average ration was about a gallon a month for adult men, half as much for women. As though to underline the*

Amana schoolhouse can be seen on the left of the photo. Grapes can be seen growing on the trellises on the side of the building, which was common in the Amana colonies. *Amana Heritage Society.*

> *connection between wine and the spirit, the colonists use the basement of their meeting house as their wine cellar.*

Winemaking was a part of culture in Germany and had a long history in Europe, so when the Inspirationists finally came to America, they brought these traditions and knowledge with them. Even though they were very strict about certain societal norms, they never prohibited the consumption of alcohol.

In 1843, the Inspirationists came to America and settled on a large tract of land in Buffalo, New York, that became known as Eben-Ezer. This five-thousand-acre tract of land included six communal living communities that worked for the common good of the community without pay. In return, residents were given food, housing, clothing and anything they needed by the society that oversaw them.

The area where they settled is a popular area for vineyards today, located near the Great Lakes. However, the settlers, while planting a number of orchards, did not plant large vineyards. It was not until the Inspirationists settled in Amana, Iowa, in the 1850s that they began the practice of planting grapevines that trellised up the sides of their homes.

WINE TICKETS

In Amana, the production of wine was substantial, although in the early years it was considered communal and placed in the society's wine cellars. Everything produced in the community was for the entire society to use. Wine was no exception, but it was regulated a bit. Each person was given an allotment of wine per year. This allotment varied a bit from year to year. On average, an adult male was given twelve gallons and a woman received six gallons. In some years, this number reached twenty gallons per man. On average, the villages produced four thousand to eight thousand gallons of wine annually.

The allotment came in the form of a wine ticket. When a member came for wine, the ticket was punched and a recording of the distribution was made in a record book. Like in any community, not everyone wanted to drink, so members could give their tickets to relatives or friends who did drink. In addition to the society members' allotment, extra wine was given to farm crews in the field, including boys as young as fourteen.

Amana Society day laborers enjoying some time off in Amana, Iowa, circa 1915. *Amana Heritage Society.*

Wooden sidewalks and grape trellises are visible in High Amana. Photograph by William Foerstner. *Amana Heritage Society.*

On the first Monday of each month, wine was distributed to the community. In Homestead, the day for wine distribution was on the first Wednesday of the month. Each member would bring his or her ticket and jug to be filled. Even though they were allowed twelve or more gallons a year, they were limited to only two gallons a month.

In order to manage the communal wine production, the board of trustees of the Amana Society authorized a formal organization of wine cellars on September 29, 1865. The board secretary recorded, "Wine from wild grapes…should be produced on a communal basis and distributed by head-count to all communities equally. Jakob Schnetzler, Jakob Scheuner, Georg Dickel, August Koch, Jakob Kilpfel, and David Pansa have been designated to carry out this resolution and are thus notified."

Most of the villages in Amana produced grapes for the communal cellars with the exception of Homestead, which produced rhubarb wine. Each community had its own wine masters. The vineyards ranged from three to six acres, and most were planted on south-facing slopes. The vines were planted from six to seven feet apart, and the rows were also six to seven feet

Above: This circa 1910 view of the village of Middle Amana was taken from the woolen mill, looking northeast. A portion of the terraced Middle Amana vineyard is visible at center. *Amana Heritage Society.*

Right: Dr. Christian Herrman photographed this child with grapes in the early 1900s. Nearly all the villages had homes and buildings with grape arbors. The Amanas are noted for wine production. *Amana Heritage Society.*

apart. The grape varieties they planted were Concord, Catawba, Worden and Clinton.

In addition to the vineyards, grapes were also grown on trellises around the homes. These grapes were used for home use, not for communal wine. The trellises also provided shade for the houses during the summer months and helped cool the homes. Whatever grapes were not eaten were placed on a wagon that stopped by the homes to be added to the communal harvest to make wine. As the vines were growing into maturity during the 1860s, wild grapes were harvested from the Iowa River Valley.

Harvesting the Grapes

Growing and harvesting grapes was a big deal in the Amana villages. During the fall harvests, the entire village would turn out. Children were let out of school for the day, and all other chores and work was suspended for the adults. The members of the village would work together to harvest the grapes, and those not picking would produce a picnic, which was the only interruption in the long day of harvesting.

The grapes were gathered in willow baskets that had handles on each end. The handles were strapped to the pickers through their belts so that they would have their hands free to pick grapes. Once the grapes were harvested into the baskets, they would be placed on a wagon to be hauled to the village press house. The village press house was usually next to the village wine cellar. The juice was pressed and siphoned into large vats using pipes that led to the wine cellar, which was underground.

The wine cellar in Homestead was in a large room under the west end of the community church building. The press house was in the yard directly behind the church. The community vineyard in Homestead was in the field next to the church. In High Amana, the wine cellar was in the large basement of the village school. In Middle Amana, the village vineyard was planted on a series of terraces on the side of the hill on which the village stood. The wine cellar was located beneath a building used for small prayer meetings that later became part of the first Amana High School Building after the 1932 reorganization. The East Amana vineyard was located on the north side of the village, with the wine cellar again beneath the church building. This wine cellar alone contained huge five-hundred-gallon barrels. In order for the barrels to be used from year to year, one of the boys from

A typical sandstone building in Amana. It was common to plant grapevines on the sides of the buildings and build a trellis to allow them to grow up. This was for practical reasons as well as aesthetic. Circa 1938. *Amana Heritage Society.*

the village would have to crawl inside to scrape off the tartaric acid that had crystalized on the walls from the last wine that had aged there.

The Amana press house was a shed behind the church. Once the grapes were harvested and brought to the press house in large tubs, they were pressed through a two-roller masher to break them and help remove some of the stems. The grapes were then put into a large screw press to expel the juice.

TYPES OF WINE

The press in Amana was rather large, standing at five feet tall. It took two men to operate the screw. The wine from the first press, called *vorlauf*, was a lighter wine that was made into the wine for distribution to the members of the community for their allotment.

A man using a wine thief to test large fermenting wine barrels at a winery in Amana, circa 1906. *Amana Heritage Society.*

The juice from this first press ran down into large tanks, and then in the cellar, the juice was siphoned into the large wooden wine casks. Some of them held as much as one thousand gallons of wine. This vorlauf wine was usually made from Concord and Worden grapes. Here is the recipe for creating this community wine:

> *10 gallons of grape juice*
> *20 pounds of sugar*
> *The sugar was dissolved in water before being added to the juice. The mixture was added to the wine casks using this formula proportion until it was full.*

As mentioned earlier, the members of the villages grew other varieties of grapes. Catawba grapes were reserved for communion (Liebesmahl) services. This wine was only produced in the Amana village, as members from the surrounding villages would come to Amana for communion service. The recipe for this communion wine was:

For every 10 gallons of wine
3 gallons of juice
20 pounds of sugar dissolved into water.

Wines made from wild grapes made in Amana used the following recipe:

For every 10 gallons of wine
4 gallons of juice
20 pounds of sugar dissolved into water.

Once the grapes were pressed and the sugar and water added, the juice was allowed to ferment for a week to ten days with the grape skins still present. This was sent back through the press for the second press, or *tresterwein*. This wine was redder because the tannins and color were released from the skins. Two more gallons of sugar were added to the wine must (fermenting grape juice) and allowed to ferment. The wine continued to ferment through early spring, and once it was beginning to clear, it was siphoned off the lees (sediment in the bottom) into a new cask.

If you have tasted wine from Amana or a lot of wineries in the Midwest, you will realize that they are often sweet. Additional sugar is added to the wine after it has stopped fermenting in a process known as chaptalization. This process was not used in their native Germany; rather, they picked it up in the United States. In the fruit wines, sugar was added to counteract bitterness and add some body to the wine.

RHUBARB WINE

You can make wine from just about any fruit or vegetable with varying amounts of success. Rhubarb (piestengel) was a very popular wine that is still made in Amana today and is just as popular now as it was in the nineteenth century. Another popular choice was dandelion wine, made from the young plants in early spring. These wines were made in the home rather than for communal use. As mentioned earlier, a lot of extra sugar was added not only for flavor but also because it was necessary for fermentation, as these fruit wines often lacked natural sugars like those in grapes.

Above: Les Ackerman and his nephew Jacob Wendler carrying a basket of rhubarb that will be crushed and processed into their famous rhubarb wine using an old-world recipe. *Linda Ackerman Collection.*

Left: Carrie Ackerman tending to a rhubarb plant on the Ackerman farm, June 1983. *Linda Ackerman Collection.*

The rhubarb grown in Amana could grow as high as five feet tall with leaves twenty inches wide. When ready, the stalks were pulled, not cut from the plant, as a way to preserve the juice.

PROHIBITION OF WINE

As you may have deduced, creating wine at home was a way to get around the limited amount of grape wine allotted to residents. The council caught on and tried to get rhubarb wine production under control. At a council meeting on April 6, 1897, it was declared, "No rhubarb is to be planted or raised in the community other than two or three plants per kitchen garden for pie or sauce, but not for wine."

The efforts to stop home wine production failed. Many homes had a room called a *wein stobe* or wine room in their cellars where they sat and drank and

Men testing and drinking wine at a winery facility in the Amana Colonies. The man in the middle is holding a wine thief. This was like a long turkey baster inserted into a barrel that extracted wine in order to be tasted and tested. *Amana Heritage Society.*

entertained friends. The way wine was being produced and consumed was not only an issue for the members within the colonies, but some sought to profit from it.

In a meeting of the board of trustees on January 6, 1868, the minutes read:

> *Since we have become aware that members have privately sold cigars, tobacco, wine, young grapevines, berry shrubs and flowering plants for personal profit, we hereby remind all that no such private business is permitted. If we sell tobacco and cigars to day workers, we can get into serious trouble. Taxes have to be collected, and by not doing so, we can be severely penalized.*

The issue of homemade wine continued to vex community leaders. In a meeting of the board of trustees on June 21, 1869, it was noted, "We must also caution our members that wine, etc. be consumed in moderation only, avoiding revelry and intemperance."

In 1878, the board of trustees finally created an ultimatum and forbade the members to make wine at home at all. This did have an effect on wine sales and wine consumption, so it has remained as a communal regulation since that time.

The winemakers in Amana, while supportive of temperance, were not necessarily in favor of total prohibition. They did, however, believe in following the laws of the land. In 1884, the Iowa state legislature passed a prohibition law that abolished the production of liquor in the state. The board of trustees responded by drafting an essay to all members of the society that stated:

> *The wine too we must seek to sell so that the community cellars will be empty by that date* [July 4]. *What cannot be distributed by then or what individual members still have in their own possession must be conscientiously and legally dealt with. Whether wine may once again be produced in the future remains to be seen, at the moment the law forbids it.*
>
> *Since we are obligated to obey the law, we hereby stress particularly that all members must absolutely avoid offending in any way whatsoever. We also wish to make everyone aware that the community cannot and will not accept responsibility under any circumstances. Should anyone be found guilty in spite of these warnings, the offender must personally accept full blame and personally bear the penalty and punishment.*

A large basket press outside a building in Middle Amana. There is a grape arbor on the side of the building. *Amana Heritage Society.*

Even with members pleading to the state supreme court for some resolutions, the restrictions held. The trustees ordered the grapes harvested, turned into jellies and syrup and distributed among the members. In 1895, some reprieve came in the passage of the Mulct Law, which allowed individual counties to declare whether they were wet or dry. The Amana villages were able to produce wine for a time, but the prohibition issue would continue for many more years both locally and nationally.

The issue of home winemaking was still at the top of the minds of trustees, as they could not see to get a foothold. On September 1, 1896, they stated to members of the colonies:

> *It is being empathically repeated that making wine from grapes, wild or domestic or from anything else, is strictly forbidden and must remain so. Whoever does it in spite of this ruling is not for the preservation and edification of our community, but for its decay and destruction. What brings on these transgressions? The excessive passion and lust for the wine which then only cause body and soul to suffer or even die. Or else it is the craving for money, whereby the sin is doubled or tripled through the sale of the wine, plus the trouble it then causes and has caused elsewhere, almost leading to murder even, and all this as a result and fully resting upon the conscience and responsibility of the one who produced the wine in the first place.*

As mentioned elsewhere in this book, weather in the Midwest was a serious factor in growing grapevines. In 1899, a severe winter destroyed a large

These young women from Main Amana were photographed in 1913 by Cedar Rapids photographer John H. Richmond, who signed his work "J Rich." The trellises covering the walls of the house behind the women are typical of the grape trellises found on virtually every home in the communal era. *Amana Heritage Society.*

portion of the community vineyards. The council turned a blind eye in some ways to wine production, but in 1911, federal authorities were not so merciful. The federal tax authorities had become aware of wine being sold in the villages and decided to investigate. At that time, it was not illegal to produce wine, but it was illegal to sell without paying the proper taxes.

The outcome of the investigation was that members were caught selling wine and were forced to pay a penalty, but then they received a license to allow them to sell more wine legally in the future. The trustees were not happy with this outcome and wanted the licenses destroyed. In their meeting, they declared, "To what purpose are such persons in the Community, except…to devastate God's community and turn it into a house of imbibing and indeed of drunkenness so that, in the end, all abomination is practiced?"

WORLD WAR I

During World War I, the cost of sugar increased, and therefore, communal winemaking decreased. The trustees once again made their point known that there should be no home winemaking.

World War I was not kind to this German colony. Neighbors in communities surrounding the colonies were very suspicious of the members. First, they were native Germans who spoke German. They also refused to bear arms in the military. This led to editorial attacks on the society in the newspapers, along with threats of mob violence. This made the trustees and leaders of the colonies very nervous. The leaders wanted to assure those around them that they were no threat and they just wanted to be respected members of the larger community.

New prohibition laws went into effect on July 4, 1917, in Iowa. The trustees once again demanded compliance with the new laws of their members. If a member was found guilty of violating the laws, the society would not defend his or her actions. The trustees had the grapes on hand turned into vinegar and ordered the destruction of nineteen thousand gallons of wine. Casks were broken open with axes into drainage ditches. The Iowa River ran red with wine.

It was not enough to destroy the wine; the trustees ordered the destruction of the vines and vineyards. The only grapes that were allowed to be saved were those growing on trellises on the sides of residences. These grapes could be used for eating and cooking only. Even with this overt compliance

A view of the Upper South Hotel looking north in Amana Colonies, circa 1930s. There are grapes growing in the vineyard next to the hotel. *Amana Heritage Society.*

with the laws, the trustees felt that fines and imprisonment were too harsh of a punishment under Prohibition.

A few years later, the Eighteenth Amendment was passed, which took Prohibition to a national level. There have been rumors that even during Prohibition, winemaking bootleggers existed in Amana. Two members were arrested and fined. The trustees expelled one of these members from the society.

The Great Depression beginning in 1929 increased pressure on the society, and many of the members became disillusioned. The society as a whole was having financial problems. The members voted to abandon the communal living model and created a joint stock corporation, the Amana Society. The organization would handle their business affairs, and another organization, the Amana Church Society, would oversee their religious life.

Under this restructuring, members received stock and were able to purchase their own homes and receive wages for their work. All other communal functions such as communal kitchens were terminated. This change occurred on June 1, 1932, at which time the Volstead Act was still in effect. The communal wine cellars were never reopened after 1917; however, when Prohibition was repealed, some residents went into the commercial wine business.

EHRLE BROTHERS

In 1934, brothers Emil Ehrle (1901–1951) and William Ehrle Jr. (1902–1969) began to produce wine commercially. It was the first commercial wine venture in Amana following the communal wine years. Emil was a wool buyer for the Amana Woolen Mill while his younger brother William was the manager of the Homestead General Store. The winery was named Ehrle Brothers Winery, and it began just as a hobby wine business. The Ehrle

When the farmers brought in the grapes to the Council Bluffs Grape Growers Association, the fruit immediately went into the destemming and crushing machine. Charles Herrill is seen here pouring grapes into the machine. In 1943, farmers received eighty dollars a ton for grapes, whereas in 1942 they only received sixty dollars. September 19, 1943. *Des Moines Register.*

Right: Emile Ehrle siphons sweet, ruby-red wine made from grapes into jugs to be sold in Amana, Iowa. Photograph by Jervas Baldwin, October 7, 1945. *Des Moines Register.*

Below: Winery interior, Amana, Iowa, 1950s, with Marvin Krauss and Carl Christen. Barrels are moved, and wine is then siphoned into bottles. The barrels can only be used a few times before they are discarded. Over time, the staves can shrink and the barrels will leak. Photograph by William F. Noe. *Amana Heritage Society.*

brothers operated under a special permit issued by the Iowa State Liquor Control Commission that only allowed them to produce and sell a total of 1,000 gallons per year. The Ehrles sold this wine in jugs for four dollars a gallon. In 1945, the Ehrles produced only 850 gallons because a late frost damaged their Concord grapes.

After Emil died in 1949, his wife, Alma (1904–1984), took over the business. With the help of her husband's longtime assistant Chris Hergert (1903–1985), she was able to keep the vineyard going. They expanded the original winery, producing rhubarb wine (piestengel) in the spring and grape wine in the fall. Using the original formula for wine served during the Amana communion (Liebesmahl or "love feast"), Ehrle Brothers produced what it marketed as "Lover's Wine."

Originally, the Ehrles bought their grapes from Amana residents and then from vineyards in the Cedar Rapids area. Due to vineyards being hurt from 2,4-D (a toxic herbicide), they had to obtain their grapes from Nauvoo, Illinois. The Ehrles bottled their wine in quart-sized stoneware jugs, and their wine cellar was the basement of the Ehrle home.

After Alma passed, her daughter and son-in-law, Lynda and Arthur Miller, sold the business to Les Ackerman of South Amana. Ackerman continued to produce wine under the Ehrle name. In 1989, the Ackermans sold the business to the Krauss family, who operated the winery for the next twenty-six years. In 2015, Ehrle Brothers Winery, the oldest in the state of Iowa, closed its doors.

THE OLD-STYLE COLONY WINERY

Almost fifteen years later, a second commercial winery in the Amana villages was founded by entrepreneur George Kraus (1921–2011) in 1949. Kraus, who had learned winemaking from his grandfather, named his winery the Old-Style Colony Winery. Like the Ehrles, Kraus began with his winery in his home in Middle Amana, which was the meat market before being purchased by the Kraus family in 1934. Kraus added a tasting room and other facilities to the home.

Kraus experimented with different types of fruit beyond the traditional grape, rhubarb and dandelion. He produced country wines made from tomatoes, red clover, blueberries, oranges, cranberries and grapefruit—over twenty-five varieties in all. Some were successes, others not so much.

Winery interior, Amana, Iowa, 1950s, with Marvin Krauss and Carl Christen. Marvin is testing the barrels that contain wine that is aging. Cellars are underground so that the wines can remain cool and stable without danger of refermenting or contamination. Photograph by William F. Noe. *Amana Heritage Society.*

By 1984, the Kraus family had sold their home and the winery to Michael and Pamela Schmitz and family from Des Moines. The Schmitzes operated the winery until the early 1990s, when it was closed and the building was converted back into a family home.

Ackerman Winery

In 1956, Harry (1922–2011) and Louisa (1922–1989) Ackerman and Harry's father, Herman (1892–1965), began producing wine in the basement of the 1867 former kitchen house occupied by the family in South Amana. During the summer months, all four of the Ackermans assisted in the winemaking process.

Harry Ackerman mixing and crushing fruit in a large basket press to be squeezed into juice, which was then fermented into wine. Ackerman Winery, Amana, Iowa, 1956. *Linda Ackerman Collection.*

They used four small basket presses with hydraulic jacks to extract juice, which was then poured into repurposed oak whiskey barrels (later replaced by plastic tanks) for aging. The wine was racked from barrel to barrel multiple times as a natural filtration process.

The bottles were then filled with a plastic tube siphon from the barrels. The Ackermans did not experiment in the early days and only made grape and rhubarb wine. They suggested that customers could mix the two and create an "Amana cocktail." The alcohol content of the rhubarb wine reached as high as 20 percent.

Manual basket press used at Ackerman Winery to squeeze juice out of fruit and plants such as rhubarb. The pressure is gradually increased until all of the juice is extracted, a process that can take a couple of hours. Sugar, yeast and other additives are then added to must (fermenting juice) and placed in a fermenter. *Linda Ackerman Collection.*

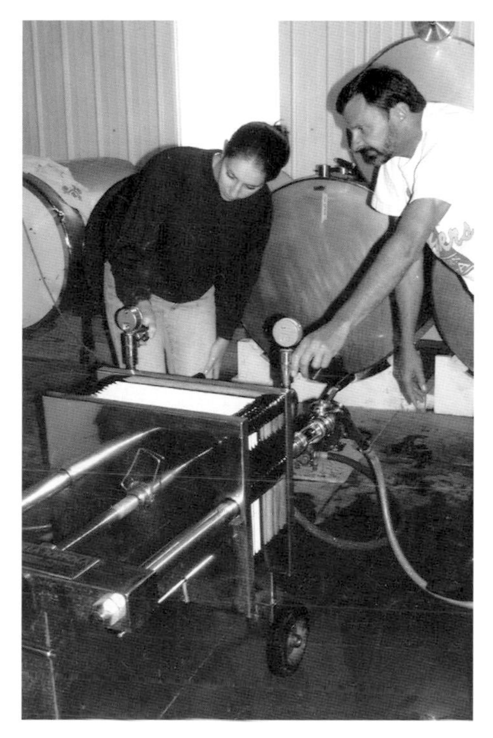

Left: Les and Greta Ackerman making adjustments to the plate and frame filter system. Wine is pressurized and passes through the filters to improve color and taste as well as remove debris or anything that could spoil the wine. Sheet filters are placed in frames, and the wine is pushed through them. *Linda Ackerman Collection.*

Below: Les Ackerman taking a trip to Pekin, Illinois, in preparation for the fall harvest, winemaking and barrel aging. August 1974. *Linda Ackerman Collection.*

Wine was sold by the jug. Harry Ackerman is showing off his wines in his small winery in Amana, Iowa, 1956. *Linda Ackerman Collection.*

In 1974, the Ackermans' son Les purchased the business and adjacent home. Les was a bit more experimental and expanded the varieties offered to about twenty-one. He also began using plate, frame and cartridge filters in the process and used an eight-spigot gravity filler in the bottling process. Les did not rely on natural processes that could sometimes result in spoiled wine and opted to use preservatives. He also converted the aging process to stainless steel tanks. Eventually, the Ackermans also added a retail cheese shop in an existing building on the property.

In 1984, the Ackermans expanded their business by creating Heritage Haus Wine and Cheese in the village of Amana. Heritage Haus began as an independent winery, housed in the former watchmaker and tin shop, leased

Harry Ackerman testing the wine as it ferments and ages in oak barrels. The wine is drawn out and tasted and tested in a lab. Ackerman Winery, Amana, Iowa, 1956. *Linda Ackerman Collection.*

from sisters Betty Lou Griess and Mary Ann Fels, until they sold it to the Ackermans in 2004. In later years, the Heritage Haus ceased to exist, and the business became an outlet for the Ackerman Winery.

In 2000–01, the Ackermans fulfilled a longtime dream of having a self-guided winery tour by converting a residence that had once been the communal-era Amana village bakery into the new home of the Ackerman Winery. The Ackermans were proud of the fact that despite having to transfer fifty stainless steel tanks, ranging in size from 150 to 600 gallons, and 14,000 gallons of wine from South Amana to Amana, the business was closed for only one day during the move.

The Ackermans finally retired in 2014 and sold the winery and Heritage Haus to the Wyant family of rural Marengo.

Right: Winemaking was a family affair. Greta Ackerman, daughter of Harry Ackerman, with a fermentation bucket. Ackerman Winery, Amana, Iowa. *Linda Ackerman Collection.*

Below: Linda Ackerman on a trip to Pekin, Illinois, posing with the barrels they have collected to use at the Ackerman Winery, August 1974. *Linda Ackerman Collection.*

SANDSTONE WINERY

A fourth Amana winery, the Sandstone Winery, was founded in 1960 by Joseph "Jodie" (1915–1999) and Elsie (1922–2010) Mattes. Like the others, it began in the basement of their family home, which was a former communal kitchen house.

A 1975 article in the *Cedar Rapids Gazette* featured the Mattes family as they made piestengel. At the time, they used a crusher with a patent date of 1866 and had eight thousand gallons of piestengel, grape and cherry wine. Following Jodie Mattes's death in 1999, Stumpff and Elise Mattes continued to operate the winery. Elsie Mattes died in 2010. Today, the winery is operated by her daughter and son-in-law.

OLD WINE CELLAR

Ramon Goerler (1928–2006) started his winery, the Old Wine Cellar, in the basement of his family home in 1961. Goerler was a nephew of Alma Ehrle. In the 1980s, Goerler relocated his business to an 1857 residence that also contained the communal-era village shoe shop. Following Goerler's retirement in 1996, the business was operated by Barbara Buchanan of Williamsburg. In 2004, Buchanan sold the business to the Ackerman family, which maintained the Old Wine Cellar label for a year, after which the retail space became an outlet for Ackerman Winery. In 2007, the Ackermans sold the building to the Cutler family of Amana, who have since operated it as a clothing store.

LITTLE AMANA WINERY

The Little Amana Winery was founded by brothers-in-law Kenneth Schaefer (1926–2012) and Elmer Kraus (1924–2006) of East Amana, in partnership with Arthur Miller of the Ehrle Brothers Winery. This winery operated from a building located at the Interstate 80 interchange near Amana, known as "Little Amana." It opened on June 19, 1971, and grew into the largest winery in the state of Iowa for over twenty years. When Schaefer retired in 1997, his longtime employee Robert Zuber and wife Mary purchased the business and continued to operate it for many years. The business closed with Zuber's retirement in 2009, and the space is now occupied by the Village Winery, operated by the Krauss family.

Der Weinkeller (the Wine Cellar)

In 1974, the same partnership behind the Little Amana Winery opened Der Weinkeller ("the Wine Cellar"), located in the basement of the former Amana doctor's office and pharmacy building, constructed in 1867. The winery produced dandelion, rhubarb, cherry, peach and raspberry fruit wines and Johannesburg, Riesling, Chein Blanc and Catawba grape wines. Schaefer retired in 1997 and sold the business to Robert and Mary Zuber. In 2004, the Zubers closed the business, concentrating their winemaking at the Little Amana Winery. The Kraus family leased the original winery space and opened the Village Vintner.

Colony Village Winery

The Colony Village Winery was a partnership between the Ackerman and Roemig families. This winery operated from the basement of the Colony Village Restaurant, which was owned and operated by the Russel Sandersfeld family. The founders of the Village Winery came from a long tradition of family winemaking. The Krauss family's experience in winemaking extended back to Louis Krauss (1861–1938), one of the communal winemakers.

In 1973, Louis's grandson Don; his wife, Eunice; and their sons Don Jr. and Ray opened their winery in a modern building between the Amana Furniture Shop and the Amana Woolen Mill. Today, Village Winery produces approximately fifteen different types of wine. Through the years, the Krauss family acquired and operated Ehrle Brothers, Der Weinkeller and the Little Amana Winery. The Krauss family of the Village Winery and the Kraus family of the Old Style Winery share a similar last name but are not related.

Grape Vine Winery

After a fifty-year-long career at the Amana Meat Shop, George Schuerer (1918–2012) of East Amana opened the Grape Vine Winery in an 1873 residence adjacent to the Meat Shop in the 1980s. Schuerer learned winemaking from his father and grandfather and offered approximately sixteen different varieties of wine.

In later years, wine production at the Grape Vine was under the direction of Les Haldy. Following Haldy's death and due to the declining health and age of its owners, Grape Vine ceased operations around 2008.

White Cross Cellars

David Rettig of Middle Amana worked in Der Weinkeller as a high school student. He and his wife, Mary, shared a loved for wine and wine culture and opened the White Cross Cellars in a former retail space across from the Amana Furniture Shop. David had been in the furniture retail business for many years.

The Amana winemaking tradition continues to persist long after the communal system and the original winemakers are gone. Today, modern equipment, techniques and formulas are carrying the Amana wine tradition into the twenty-first century. Many permanent Amana residents continue to produce their own wines such as piestengel in small batches in their home basements, just as their forebearers did.

Note: Much of the information gathered in this chapter came from *Winemaking in the Amana Colonies*, written by Peter A. Hoehnle, PhD, and was commissioned and used by permission of Wilrona, LLC and Ackerman Winery.

Chapter 6

CHALLENGES OF GROWING IN IOWA

There are different man-made and environmental pressures that impact not only the growing of grapes but also making wine and selling it. In 1899, Iowa was ranked eleventh in grape production in the nation. In 1919, it was ranked sixth, and while there were many factors in favor of grape growing in Iowa, there were also obstacles it faced. Some challenges took time and tenacity to overcome. Some factors, though, led to the death of the wine industry for almost forty years.

Grape growing is different than other types of crops. The federal government does not subsidize grape growing or winemaking. Iowa has the nation's third highest excise tax at $1.75 per gallon on all wholesale sales of wine.

In 1860, the eighth census of the U.S. government said this about viticulture in the United States:

> *Disease, insects, and frost.—The grape, like other fruits, has it enemies. The most destructive of these is the mildew or rot. Was it not for this disease the Catawba would be immensely profitable; but of late years, in the Ohio valley, it has destroyed from one-fifth to four-fifths of the crop in many vineyards, and discouraged some persons from planting that fine grape. A sudden change of weather from hot to cold when the vine is in rapid growth, and the seed in the berries about hardening, is sure to produce rot. A free under-drainage—either natural or artificial—and a full exposure to the wind, will in part prevent it. No system of pruning or cultivation has yet proved a sufficient remedy in vineyards. Vines trained against the side of*

> *a house, and under cover of the eaves, seldom, if ever, rot. The disease probably results from atmospheric causes, as the rust in wheat.*
>
> *Insects have not as yet been found very injurious, but the careful vine-dresser will watch closely, and permit none to get colonized in his vineyard. The frost in some localities kills the young shoots of the vine in April, or early in May, but the twin or latent bud will put out, and yield about half a crop. To prevent serious injury by hail, let the bunches of grapes be well sheltered by the leaves of the vine, which will also prove a protection from the hot sun.*

The 1900 U.S. agricultural census showed that Iowa produced 7,403,900 pounds of grapes and produced 76,201 gallons of farm-processed wine.

Council Bluffs District

The Council Bluffs district had some advantages over other places in Iowa. While there were a few winters in which there was severe damage to vines, they were rare. Since the district was located in the southwestern part of the state along the Missouri River, the climate was more temperate. In other areas, grape growers would often take the vines off the trellises, lay them down and cover them for the winter to protect them from the harsh winters, but not so in the Council Bluffs district. Some of the farmers would plow furrows toward the vines in late fall in order to protect the root systems of the vines.

Most of the rainfall in the Council Bluffs district occurred during the growing season. The soil was such that it was able to easily absorb the excess water, and there was not much problem with erosion or fungous diseases. The soil is deep and is known as Missouri loess. It is similar to the soils of the Rhine and Moselle regions in Germany, which are famous for their vineyards. There are two other places in the world with similar soil: the slopes of southern France and the Yangtze River Valley of China. Some have said other regions, such as the valley of the Nile and along the Missouri River, also boast similar soil.

Missouri loess is very fine grained and is formed by wind. It has a high percentage of plant food and lime content, which lead to its high water-holding capacity. It keeps the surface of the soil dry while providing an excellent water supply for the root system below. Because of its location and soil, during the height of early grape growing in the region, there were not many outbreaks of black rot (*Guignardia bidwellii*) or downy mildew (*Plasmopara viticola*), and so for the most part the grape growers did not spray their grapes.

There were a few pests they did have to contend with. The grape rootworm (*Fidia viticida*) was present but not too much of a problem. Grape growers would deal with the pest by plowing up the grapes in the fall and throwing away the furrows in the spring.

Another pest they had to contend with was the grape vine borer (*Schistoccrus hematas*). It was dealt with by burning the long cane prunings.

Factors That Led to the Demise of the Wine Industry

There is no one factor that led to the disappearance of the wine industry in Iowa. It was progressive, and the vineyard and winery owners fought on multiple fronts to stay alive, but eventually wine in Iowa went into a sort of dormancy from the mid-twentieth century until about the year 2000. According to Michael White, Iowa State University extension and outreach viticulture specialist, there are four main factors that combined to crush the Iowa wine industry:

- early prohibition
- the Armistice Blizzard of 1940
- herbicides
- government farm commodity programs

Early Prohibition

While Prohibition began nationally in 1920, Iowa had begun its own prohibition in 1916, four years before. Iowa was one of the strongest advocates of prohibition, alongside Kansas and Maine.

It began in 1851 when the Iowa General Assembly prohibited "dram shops," which we would now refer to as bars. This movement was begun with the political party called the Whigs. In 1882, an amendment to the state constitution made it illegal to manufacture and sell alcoholic beverages in the state, making it a "dry state." The amendment only lasted a year before the Supreme Court declared it unconstitutional. In 1883, another strict law was passed by the Iowa legislature concerning alcohol in the state. This remained in effect until 1893, when a new law, the "mulct law," came into effect, which gave local districts the power to make their own local provisions.

A large push toward the eradication of alcohol came from the Woman's Christian Temperance Union (WCTU). This group organized in Iowa in 1874, and its mission was to make liquor illegal. The organization continued strongly until the 1930s before the repeal of Prohibition. Its watchwords were agitate, educate and organize. The dues to join the WCTU were just one dollar, and members wore knotted white ribbons as a badge of membership. By 1930, they were sixty thousand strong.

The WCTU was not the only influencer in the state; there was a new political party in the 1870s called the Prohibition Party. In 1884, Iowa Republicans passed one of the first prohibition laws the state or country had seen. Other temperance groups in the state were:

- Sons of Temperance
- Order of Good Templars
- Iowa State Templar Alliance (Methodists)

Iowa's Alcohol Laws

On February 20, 1933, Congress proposed the Twenty-First Amendment, which repealed national Prohibition. After Prohibition, new laws had to be created not only on a national level but at a state level. It was not until July 10, 1933, that Iowa finally ratified the amendment, and on December 15, 1933, it was in full effect.

On March 6, 1934, the Iowa Liquor Control Act was enacted. With it, Iowa assumed control over the wholesale and retail sale of all alcoholic liquors except for beer. The act also established the Iowa Liquor Control Commission. This commission continued to be in control for the next thirty years. In 1963, the class C liquor license was created, which allowed the sale of alcoholic liquor by the glass for consumption on licensed premises. Counties were given the "local option" of prohibiting liquor by the drink in their jurisdictions. This option continued until it was eventually repealed on January 1, 1972.

In 1972, Chapter 123 was created, which streamlined the number of chapters from twelve to just one. Beer and liquor were combined under the Iowa Beer and Liquor Control Department, which replaced the Iowa Liquor Commission.

Sunday sales of liquor did not occur until 1973. New statutes allowed qualifying licensees and permittees to sell alcoholic beverages on Sunday by adding a new sales privilege. Like before, counties could decide for themselves as a local option whether to allow Sunday sales in their jurisdictions. This local option was repealed on August 15, 1977.

In the 1980s, things changed more significantly. In 1981, Iowa Alcohol Code permitted an Iowa brewer to obtain a single class B beer permit at its manufacturing site. This was a three-tier change. The permit allowed the holder to sell beer it obtained from a wholesaler for on- or off-premises consumption.

In 1985, the new three-tier system helped end Iowa's monopoly of the wholesale and retail sale of wine. A dual system of wine was created with the new wholesale and retail wine permits to qualified applicants. In addition, native wine manufacturers were required to obtain a class A wine permit. This also allowed native wine manufacturers to ship wine to purchases in and out of state. A new wine gallonage tax was imposed on all wine sold at wholesale by native wineries.

In 1986, the Iowa Beer and Liquor Control Department was renamed the Iowa Alcoholic Beverages Division, and it retained its role as the sole wholesaler of all alcoholic liquor sold in Iowa. This also pushed all wholesale wine sales into the private sector. The division continued its control over retail wine sales in state liquor stores until June 30, 1987. Iowa also began to reduce its retail operations and began issuing new class E liquor licenses to private-sector businesses.

That same year, the Iowa Wine and Beer Promotion Board was created for the purpose of promoting Iowa-made wine and beer. The board was funded by taxes levied on native Iowa beer and wine.

Microbreweries and brewpubs began popping up all over the United States, including Iowa. In 1989, a new special class A beer (beer pub) permit was created to allow holders of class C liquor licenses and class B beer permits to manufacture beer in their establishments for on-premises consumption.

Wine shipment law changed in 1996 with the enactment of the Reciprocal Shipment of Wines law, which allowed for Iowa native wineries to ship wine into other states with reciprocal shipment privilege laws to individuals twenty-one and older. However, all the wine shipments had to be for personal use only.

Ten years later, new changes came to native wineries and breweries. A class C native wine permit was created to allow native wineries and other retailers to sell native wine for consumption on licensed premises. Also, native wineries and breweries were able to share employees, provided the person had no ownership interest in either of the licensed premises.

In 2010, Iowa wine laws turned from reciprocity to direct shipment. These new laws allowed wine manufacturers in and out of state to ship products directly to Iowa consumers for personal use upon obtaining an Iowa wine direct shipper license (twenty-five dollars per year). Wine gallonage taxes were imposed on all wine shipped to Iowa consumers.

In the next five years, more minor laws were imposed on liquor, but of note was the Iowa Code, which was amended to allow a person holding a liquor control license or retail wine or beer permit to mix and store cocktails that are not for immediate consumption. There were label requirements for storage containers, and they could not be stored in their original container. As of June 2012, there were twenty-six different wholesale wine distributors operating in Iowa.

Some laws that are unique to Iowa are:

- No mandatory "Iowa" juice requirements
- Wineries are not inspected by Iowa food inspectors; the federal government does it
- Twenty-five-dollar license to have a wine festival
- Retailers can sell Iowa wine by the bottle and have tastings if they obtain a twenty-five-dollar-per-year license
- Law allows people to take home opened wine bottles ("Wine Doggy Bag Law")
- Iowa wineries can sell beer
- Micro-distilleries can taste and sell at retail locations
- Wineries and land associated with winery are assessed for tax purposes as agricultural

ARMISTICE BLIZZARD OF 1940

The extratropical cyclone blizzard began on November 11 (Armistice Day). It was what is referred to as a Panhandle Hook. These are uncommon storms that occur in Texas and usually trek a northeast path toward the Great Lakes region. These are usually bad storms, and this one was no exception. It cut a one-thousand-mile-wide track from Kansas to Michigan. It dumped twenty-seven inches of snow in some areas in forty-eight hours. It resulted in $2.2 million in damage and claimed 145 lives. The damage to vineyards was terminal. Eighty-mile-per-hour winds and the weight of the snow crushed and broke vines and vineyards.

This was not the first time that a bad winter hit the grape industry in Iowa. In 1898, a particularly bad winter devastated vineyards. In an article in the *Des Moines Register* in July 1899 titled "Grapes and Apples Have Suffered Most Severely," Secretary Green of the State Horticultural Society reported:

> *Grapes especially have suffered severely, and it is safe to say that the state's production will not nearly equal the home demand for two or three years at least. The curious part of it is that the north part of the state suffered the least damage, while the central portion was most seriously damaged. This is probably due to the fact that in the north part they had much more snow than in the south. This protected the roots, not only of grapes, but of trees and all kinds of vines and bushes.*

In 1899, the grapes in Pottawattamie County and those in surrounding counties were the hardest hit. Growers were only able to save about 5 percent of their crop that year. They had to replant entire vineyards and wait another two years for any kind of grape crops. Even those vineyards in the southern parts of Iowa were down about 15 percent from their usual crops.

Herbicides

It is important to learn from our past so that we can avoid the same mistakes in the future. Pesticides have been an ongoing issue for many years, as they can destroy a vineyard quickly and completely. Grapevines are very sensitive to 2,4-D and dicamba (phenoxy type), herbicides used to kill broadleaves in lawns, crops, pastures and roadside ditches.

The pesticide 2,4-D was developed during World War II. It was developed to kill rice and potato crops in order to starve out Germany and Japan. It did not work because these crops were resistant to it. After the war, it was released as a broadleaf herbicide to be used around crops such as rice.

During the Vietnam War, it was a component in Agent Orange and was sprayed over patches of jungle as an herbicide and defoliant. However, another component of Agent Orange, 2,4,5-T, caused many adverse health effects to those exposed to it.

The problem is that when grapevines are exposed to the herbicide, they wilt and die. 2,4-D is produced in two forms. One is a salt and the other is an ester, which is a combination of an alcohol and acid. In this latter state, it easily volatizes into a vapor. Because of pesticide drift due to wind, vineyards even miles away from where it is being sprayed can be affected. While it was useful to those with row crops as a powerful herbicide, those with vineyards were adversely affected.

By 1962, grapes at the Bluff Experimental Farm near Council Bluffs were ruined by drifting 2,4-D. The herbicide was being sprayed on roadsides and used to control weeds in corn fields. The vapor was drifting five to ten miles in some cases. In an article in the *Des Moines Register*, "Iowa's Grapes Damaged by Drifting 2,4-D Vapor," Winton Etchen, secretary-treasurer of the Iowa Horticulture Society, said, "Since 1952 it [2,4-D] has resulted in untold financial losses to many growers and had become a direct threat to the continuation of many horticultural enterprises."

The production of the Council Bluffs Grape Growers Association dropped from 1.9 million pounds of grapes to 304,544 pounds in 1950. Because the herbicides affected the vines, the harvest period was delayed; it was about a month later than it was in 1949.

The use of the herbicide was becoming a real issue for the grape growing industry in the early 1960s. In May 1963, the Iowa Department of Agriculture prohibited the use of high-volatile forms of 2,4-D and 2,4,5-T in the western half of Pottawattamie County and all of Harrison, Mills, Lee and Muscatine Counties. This decision came on the heels of the Council Bluffs report that it had the worst grape harvest in its history.

Iowa grape growers saw an increase in their crop in 1964, and farmers claimed it was due to the ban of the weed killer. The harvest was earlier than it had been in years. The crop was so good that in 1964, growers were able to get $120 a ton, which was up $20 a ton from the previous year. But the state was not out of the woods quite yet.

A call for a state ban of the herbicide came in 1967. The 1963 pesticide law allowed Iowa secretary of agriculture L.B. Liddy to have a public hearing, and if he determined the herbicide was harmful to crops, he could ban 2,4-D. The ban on the counties in the west was not enough to stop the widespread damage of the herbicide because winds could still cause drift damage. The other challenge was that Nebraska, to the immediate west, had no ban on 2,4-D.

The statewide ban was not instituted. There was disagreement over whether it should be banned by plant scientists. In an article titled "2,4-D Is Still Haunting Iowa Grape Growers" in the *Des Moines Register* on December 6, 1970, Dr. E.L. Denison, head of the horticulture department at Iowa State University, stated, "That would be moving backward. I would hate to see the orchards and fields of Iowa if all the use of 2,4-D were suddenly halted."

There was one solution that had been offered, and it began in the western grape counties where there had been a ban: only low-volatile 2,4-D could be sold or used in the counties of Mills, Harrison and West Pottawattamie and the east counties of Muscatine and Lee. This compromise came too late, and the damage to the industry made it tough to come back. The issue of the use of 2,4-D is still one that affects vineyards and continues to be highly debated.

Government Farm Commodity Programs

As mentioned earlier, the government does not subsidize any grape growing or winemaking. The USDA began subsidizing farms for row crops. As the floor began falling out of the grape industry in Iowa, farmers began planting more row crops, as they were less risky. The days of making fortunes growing grapes were in the past, and newer generations had the choice to either sell their land or turn to more lucrative crops. The vineyard land sold was quickly turned over to row crops such as corn and soybeans. The golden age of vines in the prairie had come to an end.

Chapter 7

VINEYARD REVIVAL

In the early 2000s, grape growing came back to Iowa. In 2000, there were about 30 acres of grapes in production, while in 2018, the number is four hundred times that amount. In 2009, the largest AVA (American Viticultural Area), covering 29,914 square miles in Iowa, Illinois, Minnesota and Wisconsin, was approved by the Tobacco Tax and Trade Bureau. There are 238 AVAs in the United States. In 2016, the Loess Hills AVA in the Des Moines area was granted. It took five years and $50,000 in order to earn the designation. Having this AVA designation allows wineries to place it on the label, which lets the person buying the wine know that a large percent of the grapes in the wine were grown in a particular region.

According to statistics in 2011, Iowa shares about .04 percent of the United States wine production and market share. California is the largest producer of wine in the United States and makes up roughly 90 percent of all wine production. It also makes up 90 percent of wine exported from the United States. The other forty-nine states make up the other 10 percent of wine production.

In 1860, the eighth census of the U.S. government said this about viticulture in the United States:

> *VARIETIES OF GRAPES FOR THE VINEYARD*
> *These are now quite numerous, and every year adds more to the list. It will only be necessary to name a few of the most popular varieties.*

> *1. Catawba.—Nine-tenths of all our vineyards in the west and southwest are planted with this fine grape. With all its liability to rot, it continues a favorite.*
> *2. Delaware.—This hardy and delicious table grape promises to rival the Catawba for wine. It is becoming popular with some of our best cultivars. The wine is light and delicate, and preferred to the Catawba by many good judges. The Delaware is less subject to rot than that variety.*
> *3. Herbemont makes an excellent wine, but the vine is not hardy enough to be much planted.*
> *4. Norton's Seedling.—A hardy, free growing vine, but little affected by rot, makes a rich red wine like Burgundy, and is becoming quite popular.*
> *5. Schuylkill.—This old favorite of sixty years ago is now but little planted. The wine resembles claret when well made, but the vine bears light crops. It is almost free from rot.*
> *6. Isabella.—Another favorite of former years that is now but little cultivated for wine. It is deficient in saccharine matter to make still wine that will keep without adding sugar to the must or juice; but the sparkling wine from it is delicious.*
>
> *The Concord, Hartford Prolific, and some of Rogers's hybrids, appear to suit our climate, and to be free from disease, but are not yet fairly tested for wine. Grapes of recent introduction in high credit for northern cultivation are the Iona, and Adirondack, native of the State of New York, and the Creveling, a native of Pennsylvania. In the south, in addition to the Catawba, the Warren is largely cultivated, and the Scuppernong still holds the reputation it acquired sixty years ago. Other varieties are being tested which it is unnecessary to enumerate here. The varieties in the vineyards of California are said to be foreign or of foreign origin. I have no means of describing or even naming them.*

In 1947, Iowa State University (then Iowa State College) started cultivar trials and other experiments on grapes and other fruits at the Council Bluffs Experimental Fruit Farm near Council Bluffs. It created eighty-four cultivars of grapes from 1947 through 1965, with fifty-two under evaluation before the experimental site closed in 1965.

Today, there are a greater number of grapes being grown due to hybridization. Prior to 2000, Concord was the number-one cultivar of grapes in Iowa. There are wild grapes in Iowa, but they are either male or female. The male vines do not grow grapes.

White Grapes

Chardonel, Edelweiss, Frontenac Gris, La Crescent, La Crosse, Louise Swenson, Niagara, Petite Amie, Prairie Star, St. Pepin, Seyval Blanc, Swenson White, Vignoles, Brianna, Esprit

Red/Blue/Black Grapes

Catawba, Concord, Norton/Cynthiana, Frontenac, Leon Millot, Marechal Foch, Petite Pearl, St. Croix, Steuben, Swenson Red, Valiant, St. Vincent, GR-7, Marquette, Noiret, Corot Noir, Sabrevois

Growth of Wineries in Iowa

The number of wineries and amount of land used for vineyards has grown steadily over the years.

1999: 13 wineries, 15 growers/31 acres of commercial vineyards (only 2 of these wineries had vineyards)
2000: 14 wineries, 50+ growers/100+ acres of commercial vineyards
2001: 16 wineries, 100+ growers/200+ acres of commercial vineyards, approx. 51,500 gals./yr.
2002: 18 wineries, 175+ growers/350+ acres of commercial vineyards, approx. 49,000 gals./yr.
2003: 26 wineries, 200+ growers/400+ acres of commercial vineyards approx. 75,000 gals./yr.
2004: 33 wineries, 230+growers/500+ acres of commercial vineyards, approx. 111,000 gals./yr.
2005: 53 wineries, 305+ growers/600+ acres of commercial vineyards approx. 133,000 gals./yr.
2006: 68 wineries, 340+ growers/700+ acres of commercial vineyards, approx. 246,733 gals./yr.
2007: 70 wineries, 384+ growers/875+ acres of commercial vineyards, approx. 269,103 gals./yr.

2008: 72 wineries, 400+ growers/1,000+ acres of commercial vineyards, approx. 283,023 gals./yr.
2009: 76 wineries, 398+ growers/1,200+ acres of commercial vineyards, approx. 273,211 gals./yr.
2010: 86 wineries, 413+ growers/1,200+ acres of commercial vineyards, approx. 283,200 gals/yr.
2011: 92 wineries, 301 + growers/1,200+ acres of commercial vineyards, approx. 355,434 gals/yr.
2012: 96 wineries, 301+ growers/1,200+ acres of commercial vineyards, approx. 296,909 gals./yr.
2013: 95 wineries, 306+ growers/1,200+ acres of commercial vineyards, approx. 373,436 gals./yr.
2014: 101 wineries, 312+ growers/1,250+ acres of commercial vineyards, approx. 269,092 gals./yr.
2015: 97 wineries, 300+ growers/1,250+ acres of commercial vineyard, approx. 284,848 gals./yr.
2016: 109 wineries, 300+ growers/1,250+ acres of commercial vineyard, approx. 310,803 gals./yr.
2017: 115 wineries, 300+ growers/1,250+ acres of commercial vineyard, 292,474 gals./yr.

In 2010, Iowa was ranked twenty-third in wine production and fifteenth in the number of wineries. Even though wineries and tasting rooms are busy, especially during the summer months, 55.7 percent of the wine produced is sold wholesale for resale at retail locations. In fact, in 2015, 4,467,564 gallons of wine were purchased from wholesale, while 267,868 gallons were purchased by Iowans from wineries.

Lost Wineries from the Last Decade

In 2007, there were several wineries in Iowa, some of which no longer exist. There were many eager winery owners, but vineyard and winery ownership is not for the timid. The joke is if you want a little fortune in wine, start with a large one. It is the only business proposition that allows you to make $1 million by starting with $2 million. It is hard work, and sometimes great visions and intentions are just not enough. The conclusion you must have come to by this point is that the elements are at odds with the vineyard owner.

It is a war with nature that some years you win and others you don't. Some wineries have been able to weather losses while others fall into obscurity. Here is a list of some wineries that did not make it.

Bluestem Winery: Parkersburg. Owners: Vern and Bonnie Holm. Wine: Once in a Blue Moon. It was a retailer of wine and beer making. Winery is closed, but some wines are still available through grocery stores and some other outlets in the area.

Dale Valley Vineyards and Winery: Stuart. Owner: Ed Mahlstadt. The tasting room was in a turn-of-the century, one-room schoolhouse.

Ehrle Brothers Winery: Homestead. Owners: Don and Eunice Krause. Was once the oldest operating winery, established in 1934 (see chapter on Amana Colonies). Wines: grape, rhubarb, cherry, elderberry, cranberry, dandelion, plum, peach, strawberry and raspberry.

Faeth Farmstead Cider Mill and Winery: Fort Madison. The Faeth Orchards were founded in 1842. It was the oldest orchard west of the Mississippi. It had a heritage apple variety called a Yellow Transparent or Lodi Transparent that was in high demand. The farm was sold in six parcels and closed forever in 2008.

Grape Vine Winery: Amana. Owner: Amy Schuerer. Grape Vine was one of the eleven wineries that used to exist in Amana. Like many of the other Amana wineries, it made sweet fruit wines; in fact, it had 126 varieties.

Heartland Harvest Winery: Fort Madison. Owner: a small farming family. Wines: French hybrid and American varietals and country fruit wines.

John Ernest Vineyard and Winery: Tama. Owner: Kopsa family. Wines: Iowa Sunset Red, Pinot Noir, Morning Dew, Timber Ridge Red, Ernest Delight, Dry Red Zinfandel, Merlot, Semi-Sweet Chardonnay, Semi-Sweet Red Zinfandel, Lincoln Highway Red, Pinot Grigio, Riesling, Willow Mist, Dusty Road, Bohemie Blush Rosé, River Bottom Red and cranberry.

Kaiser Home Winery: Keosauqua. Owner: Joyce Kaiser Thomas. Wines: Sweet Concord, Iowa Whitetail, Brambleberry, White Lotus, Craisin Hell, By George and Ata Girl.

King's Crossing Vineyard: Glenwood. Owners: Rick and Karen Foster. Wine: Edelweiss. It had the theme of a medieval inn where an English king may have stopped on the way to his castle.

Little Amana Winery: Little Amana. Owner: Bob Zuber. Wines: Johannesburg Riesling, Chancellor, blackberry, elderberry, Concord grape, cranberry, rhubarb, raspberry, blueberry and strawberry.

Red Brick Winery: Ellston. Owners: John and Carol Moberg. Wines: Chardonel and Cynthiana. The winery and tasting room were in a two-story brick building built in 1918.

Sandstone Winery: Amana. Owner: Elsie Mattes. It was housed in 1960 in a century-old home of native sandstone. The wines were from recipes handed down through a number of generations.

Southern Hills Winery: Osceola. Owners: The Iowa Wine Cooperative. The cooperative was formed in 2002 and consisted of families in Iowa and neighboring midwestern states.

Spotted Horse Vineyards: Arcadia. Owners: Scott and Dawn Schweers, Dale and Virginia Schweers. Wines: dandelion, rhubarb, elderberry with honey, apple, pear and grape varieties: Edelweiss, LaCrosse, Concord, Catawba, Niagra and St. Pepin.

Sugar Grove Winery: Newton. Owners: Steve and Collette Hill. Wines: Grange Red, Rolling Hills Red, The Grate White, Vesper White, Jubilee Blush and Harvest Home White.

Timber Ridge Winery and Vineyard: Castana. Tom and Shirley Bruegger. Wines: Eveneing Delight, Sweet Apple, Spiced Apple, Frosty Timber, Harvest Moon, Top of the Hill, Frosty Fields White, Autumn Mist, cherry, plum, chokecherry and black raspberry.

Wallace Winery: West Branch. Owner: Dr. Edward Wallace. Wines: Blanc de Blanc, Iowa Barn White, Chardonel, Traminette, Claire de Lune, Wild Rosé, Iowa Barn Red, Chambourcin, Harmony, Joan's Cuvée and Malbec.

Whispering Hills Vineyards: Carson. Owners: Mike and Dana Killinger, Doug and Becky WonWeiht. Wines: St. Croix, Marechal Foch, DeChaunac, Biggy, Concord, Dry Apple, La Crosse, Edelweiss, Monndance, Catawba and Raspberry Dessert. The tasting room was more than one hundred years old.

White Oak Vineyards: Cambridge. Owners: Chris and Jan Harmeyer, Max and Pat Brewbaker. It grew five varieties of grapes and offered seven different wines.

Vineyards and Wineries Today

Some vineyards and winemakers that started in the early 2000s still exist, and a number of wineries have replaced those that did not make it. There

Sabrevois grapes growing and near harvest at the Tassel Ridge Winery in Leighton, Iowa, which is about an hour southeast of Des Moines. Grapes are watched and tested daily until their sugars are at their optimum level, and the grapes are then harvested, destemmed and crushed. Sabrevois is a sister variety of St. Croix with better winter hardiness. Sabrevois has a pleasant fruit flavor, does not have a lot of body or tannins and is often blended with other red hybrid varieties. *Tassel Ridge Winery.*

are more than one hundred wineries in Iowa in 2018 and approximately three hundred vineyards that cover around 1,200 acres and are considered to be part of the Upper Valley AVA. Many of the wineries are members of the Iowa Wine Growers Association, which has provided networking opportunities, education and pushes in legislation that have helped grape growers and winery owners.

Several newer wineries have taken over historic family farms, restored century-old barns and given new life to historic buildings by creating new wineries and tasting rooms in old spaces. The wineries are listed here by the part of Iowa in which they are located. Check out traveliowa.com for a more complete up-to-date list and also Iowawineandbeer.com and download its interactive map with updated lists and GPS directions.

Edelweiss grapes at Tassel Ridge Winery, Leighton, Iowa. One of the challenges in the Midwest is that grapes grown have to be cold hardy. Edelweiss is a hybrid varietal that is grape stock grown on hybridized American roots. This provides cold hardiness and disease resistance. *Tassel Ridge Winery.*

Eastern Iowa

Ackerman Winery: 4406 220th Trail, Amana. Opened in 1956 and is the state's oldest winery. Ackermanwinery.com.

Airport Road Vineyard and Winery: 2555 Lexington Avenue, Mount Pleasant. Airportroadvineyard.com.

Ardon Creek Vineyard and Winery: 2391 Independence Avenue, Letts. Located at a heritage farm. Ardoncreek.com.

Barrel Head Vineyard and Winery: 9995 Laudeville Road, Dubuque. South of Dubuque near the airport. Barrelheadwinery.com.

Brick Arch Winery: 116 West Main Street, West Branch. Has a three-story building for events and food. Brickarchwinery.com.

Brush Creek Winery: 16415 298th Avenue, Bellevue. Sweet and dry reds, white, berry and rhubarb wines. Brushcreekwinery.com.

Buchanan House Winery: 726 Green Road, Tipton. A nineteenth-century brick mansion that was converted. Buchananhousewinery.com.

Café Rosé: 119 North Washington Street, Edgewood. A small-lot producer of grape and fruit wines. Caferoseiowa.com.

Cedar Ridge Winery and Distillery: 1441 Marak Road NW, Swisher. Family-owned winery and distillery. Crwine.com.

Cedar Valley Winery: 2034 Dewberry Avenue, Batavia. French and American hybrid wines. Cedarvalleywine.com.

Christian Herschler District Winery: 6th and Green Street, Franklin. One of the oldest wineries in the state. Limestone home and stagecoach stop built in the 1840s. christianherschler.wix.com/winery.

Daly Creek Winery and Bistro: 106 North Ford Street, Anamosa. Wine and gourmet food. Open since 2004. Dalycreekwineryandbistro.com.

Dubuque Heritage Winery: 3365 Ashley Lane, Dubuque. One of the smallest boutique wineries in Iowa. www.facebook.com/DubuqueHeritageWinery.

Eagles Landing Winery: 127 North Street, Marquette. Located on the Mississippi River. Eagleslandingwinery.com.

East Grove Farms: 1878 355th Street, Salem. Eastgrovefarms.com.

Empty Nest Winery: 1352 Apple Road, Waukon. Berry wines. Emptynestwinery.com.

Engelbrecht Family Winery: 2866 270th Street, Fredericksburg. Thirteen estate wines and four fruit wines offered. Thefarmhousebb.com.

Fireside Winery: 1755 P Avenue, Marengo. Complimentary wine tastings. Firesidewinery.com.

Iowa Grape Vines Winery: 18345 55th Street, Maquoketa. Offers root beer and wine jelly in addition to wines. Iowagrapevines.com.

Jefferson County Ciderworks: 1839 200th Street, Fairfield. Wine made from apples. cider.work/#about-us-section.

Jennings Winery: 111E Elm Street, Strawberry Point. Production-only family winery. Jenningswinery.com.

Lindon Wines: 12646 Highway 61, Burlington. Single-varietal wines. Lindonwines.com.

Odessa Vineyards and Winery: 10448 77th Street, Wapello. Located between the Mississippi and Iowa Rivers. Odessavineyards.com.

Old Man's Creek Winery: 4625 Black Hawk Avenue SW, Parnell. Third-generation family vineyard. facebook.com/OldMansCreekVineyardandWinery.

Park Farm Winery: 15159 Thielen Road, Bankston. Parkfarmwinery.com.

Promiseland Winery: 39053 Great River Road, Guttenberg. Five boutiques and a place for light snack foods and pizza. Promiselandwinery.com.

Stone Cliff Winery: 600 Star Brewery Drive, Dubuque. Located in the historic Star brewery at the Port of Dubuque. Stonecliffwinery.com.

Sunset Ridge Winery: 12615 Highway 52 North, Dubuque. Family owned in the bluffs between Maquoketa and the Mississippi River. Sunsetridgewinery.com.

Sutliff Cider Company: 382 Sutliff Road, Lisbon. Sutliffcider.com.

Sweetland Farmstead Country Market and Winery: 3111 Highway 61, Muscatine. Seasonal fruits also available at the farm. Sweetlandfarmstead.com.

Tabor Home Vineyards and Winery: 3570 67th Street, Baldwin. Twenty-one-year-old vineyard in a century farm. Taborhomewinery.com.

Tycoga Vineyard and Winery: 2585 195th Street, Dewitt. Twenty different wines offered as well as brick oven pizza. Tycoga.com.

Village Winery: 752 48th Avenue, Amana. Fifteen varieties of fruit and berry wines. Thevillagewinery.com.

White Cross Cellars: 755 48th Avenue, Amana. Offers European-style wines. Whitecrosscellars.com.

Vineyard at Tassel Ridge Winery, Leighton, Iowa. This a picture in later spring when the dandelions have gone to seed. Often the rows are mowed or planted with low-growing ground cover that is mowed. The vines are often trellised using a two-cordon (arm) system. *Tassel Ridge Winery.*

The Backcountry Winery was built in a century-old barn by Preston and Amber Gable. They worked nights and weekends and completely remodeled the barn. In addition to a tasting room on the main floor, the barn's loft has been completely remodeled to host groups of up to 150 people. *Backcountry Winery.*

Wide River Winery: 106 North Cody Road, LeClaire. In four locations. Offers wine slushes. Wideriverwinery.com.

Wide River Winery: 1776 East Deer Creek Road, Clinton. Wideriverwinery.com.

Wide River Winery: 1128 Mound Street, Davenport. Wideriverwinery.com.

Winneshiek Wildberry Winery: 1966 337th Street, Decorah. Remodeled 1860s barn for events. wwwinery.com.

Wooden Wheel Vineyards: 1179 Highway 92, Keota. 150-year-old family farm. Woodenwheelvineyards.com.

Central Iowa

Annelise Winery: 15110 Highway 92, Indianola. Large venue for weddings. Annelisewinery.com.

Backcountry Winery: 3533 Fenton Avenue, Stratford. Restored one-hundred-year-old barn. Backcountrywinery.com.

Buzzed Bee Meadery: 1755 340th Street, Melbourne. Honey-based wines. Buzzed-bee-meadery.com.

The Cellar at White Oak: 15065 NE White Oak Drive, Cambridge. A number of cold-hardy grape varietal wines. Whiteoakcellar.com.

Covered Bridges Winery: 2207 170th Trail, Winterset. Views of the North River Valley. Coveredbridgeswinery.com.

Deal's Orchard Hard Cider: 1102 244th Street, Jefferson. Dealsorchard.com.

Dome Winery: 339 East Main Street, Belmond. Small-batch fruit wines. Domewinery.com.

Eagle City Winery: 28536 160th Street, Iowa Falls. Vineyard, winery and gift shop. Eaglecitywinery.com.

Fox Ridge Winery: 1465 L Avenue, Traer. Family owned with countryside views. Foxridgewine.com.

Garden Winery: 621 Thomas Street, Callender. Dry to semi-sweet wines. Gardenwinery.com.

Jasper Winery: 2400 George Flagg Parkway, Des Moines. Urban winery near downtown Des Moines. Jasperwinery.com.

La Vida Loca Winery: 7852 Jesup Street, Indianola. Wines made from grapes, fruits, vegetables and flowers. Also offers cooking wine. Lavidalocawinery.com.

Madison County Winery: 3021 St. Charles Road, St. Charles. Near the Madison County covered bridges. Madisoncountywinery.com.

Nearwood Winery: 210 East Robinson Street, Knoxville. Made from estate grapes ranging from red to white, sweet to dry. Nearwoodwinery.com.

99 Bottles Winery and Vineyard: 2695 Quail Avenue, Garner. Family-run, farm-style winery. 99bottleswinery.com.

Old Bank Winery: 200 North Main Street, Kanawha. Located in the restored Farmers State Bank building. Oldbankwinery.com.

Penoach Winery: 26759 North Avenue, Adel. Restored 1900s-era barn. Penaoch.com.

Prairie Moon Winery and Vineyards: 3801 West 190th Street, Ames. Iowa's only ice wine is offered. Prairiemoonwinery.com.

Snus Hill Winery: 2183 320th Street, Madrid. Offers live music on the lawn on Fridays and Sundays during the summer months. Snushillwine.com.

Soldier Creek Winery: 1584 Paragon Avenue, Fort Dodge. Family owned with wine that has won many awards nationwide. Soldiercreekwinery.com.

Summerset Winery: 15101 Fairfax Street, Indianola. Grape stomping and other seasonal events available. Summersetwine.com.

Tassel Ridge Winery: 1681 220th Street, Leighton. Local cheese- and wine-related gifts sold along with wine. Tasselridge.com.

Townsend Winery and Vineyard: 2138 160th Street, Hansell. Remodeled barn winery and tasting room. Townsendweinery.com.

Two-Saints Winery: 15170 20th Avenue, St. Charles. Six dry reds all from Iowa grapes. Twosaintswinery.com.

Van Wijk Winery: 802 4th Street, Sully. Renovated church with a gift shop and bistro on premises. Vanwijkwinery.com.

Vines to Wines: 684 20th Street, Des Moines. Vines from grapes grown all over the world. Vinestowinesdm.com.

Winterset Cidery: 1638 Highway 169, Winterset. Post and beam facility next to thirty varieties of heirloom, cider and dessert apple trees. Wintersetcidery.com.

Western Iowa

Bodega Victoriana Winery: 60397 Kidd Road, Glenwood. Post and beam barn in the Loess hills of western Iowa. Bodegavictoriana.com.

Breezy Hills Vineyard: 31735 Tamarack Road, Minden. Live music and panoramic views. Breezyhills.com.

Calico Skies Vineyard and Winery: 2368 Able Boulevard, Inwood. On a hilltop with views of an Iowa wildlife refuge. Calicoskieswine.com.

Corning Winery and Vineyard: 2300 Highway 148, Corning. facebook.com/corningwinery.

Country Barn Winery: 4213 Tanager Avenue, Primghar. Small winery in O'Brien County. Countrybarnwinery.com.

Danish Countryside Vines and Wines: 1425 Littlefield Drive, Exira. European-style wines. Danishcountrysidevinesandwines.com.

Innspiration Vines and Wines: 5079 180th Avenue, Linn Grove. Bed-and-breakfast with locally made wine. Innspirationretreat.com.

Little Swan Lake Winery: 1350 320th Avenue, Estherville. In the holds of northwest Iowa's Buffalo Ridge glacial area. lslwinery.com.

Loess Hills Vineyard and Winery: 1120 Old Lincoln Highway, Crescent. Loesshillsvineyardwinery.com.

Old Town Vineyard and Winery: 512 Father Dailey Drive, Ida Grove. Oldtowniawines.com.

Plum Creek Winery: 2306 16th Avenue, Algona. Family owned with a tasting room and party room. Plumcreekwines.com.

Prairie Crossing Vineyard and Winery: 31506 Pioneer Trail, Treynor. Covered patio and panoramic views. Prairiecrossingwine.com.

River Valley Orchards and Winery: 1645 220th Street, Humboldt. Grape and fruit wines. Fruits grown on site. Rivervalleyorchards.com.

Rustic River Winery and Vineyard: 3132 Rolf Avenue, Lake View. Family owned in the rural area of Lake View. facebook.com/rusticriverwv.

Santa Maria Vineyard and Winery: 218 West 6th Street, Carroll. Food such as pizza and meat and cheese platters available. Tuscan-themed winery. It is the only winery in Iowa producing altar wines approved for use by the Roman Catholic Church. Santamariawinery.com.

Sugar Clay Winery and Vineyards: 1446 240th Avenue, Thurman. A treehouse feel to the winery nestled in the Loess hills. Sugarclaywinery.com.

Train Wreck Winery: 112 North Phillips Street, Algona. Located at a refurbished railroad depot. Trainwreckwinery.com.

Tucker Hill Vineyards: 26001 Titan Road, Hinton. Views of the Floyd River Valley. Tuckerhillwine.com.

Vine Street Cellars: 17 North Vine Street, Glenwood. Urban winery in the city square of Glenwood. Produces twelve different wines. Vinestreetcellars.com.

Wabash Wine Company: 800 West Ferguson Road, Shenandoah. Wines and brick oven pizza are served. Located near the Wabash Trace bike trail. Wabashwinecompany.com.

There are some designated wine trails that allow for visiting a number of wineries in a particular area in a day:

Backroads Wine Trail: backroadswinetrail.com
Heart of Iowa Wine Trail: heartofiowawinetrail.com
I-80 Wine Trail: http: i80winetrail.com
Iowa Wine Trail: iowawinetrail.com
Loess Hills District Wine Trail: loesshillswinetrail.com
Northwest Prairie Wine Trail: www.northwestprairiewinetrail.com
Scenic Iowa Wine Trail: scenicriverswine.com
Western Iowa Wine Trail: westerniowawinetrail.com

Grape Yields

Many wineries buy their grapes from other vineyards. Grape yields can run from three to eighteen tons per acre with an average yield typically in the three to four tons per acre range. Grapes grown in Iowa are typically planted in ten-foot-wide rows with vines planted eight feet apart. This translates into about 545 vines per acre.

The average cost for wineries to buy their grapes from vineyards is about $1,000 to $1,400 per ton, including delivery to the winery. On average, one ton of grapes will yield about 140 to 160 gallons of juice. This might seem like a lot, but one ton of grapes will result in about two barrels of wine. Each of the barrels contains 60 gallons of wine, which is about 25 cases or 300 bottles of wine. So, a ton of grapes will yield 60 cases or about 720 bottles of wine. It takes about 500 grapes to produce one 750-milliliter bottle of wine. Also consider that it takes between 150 and 200 hours of labor a year to produce a crop in Iowa.

In addition to wineries, there are three grape juice processors in Iowa:

- Iowa Grape Vines in Maquoketa
- John 15 Vineyard in Scranton
- Moon Valley Vineyards in Oskaloosa

The Mid-America Wine Competition was started in 2007 and is held at Des Moines Area Community College (DMACC) in Ankeny, Iowa. The competition is open only to commercial wineries of Arkansas, Illinois, Indiana, Iowa, Kansas, Kentucky, Michigan, Minnesota, Missouri, Montana, Nebraska, North Dakota, Ohio, Oklahoma, Pennsylvania, South Dakota, Tennessee and Wisconsin.

IOWA WINE GROWERS ASSOCIATION

The Iowa Wine Growers Association (IWGA) is one of the largest contributors to the success of grape growing and winemaking in Iowa in the twenty-first century. IWGA is one of five viticulture associations in Iowa. The other four are smaller regional organizations, whereas IWGA covers the entire state. The other four are Northwest Iowa Grape Association, Mississippi Valley Grape Growers Association, the Western Iowa Grape Growers Association and the Scenic Rivers Grape and Wine Association.

In early 2000, the Iowa Grape Growers Association was established by the Department of Agriculture. By early 2001, it had its first annual meeting with two hundred people in attendance. In 2004, the Iowa Grape Growers Association became the Iowa Wine Growers Association, which it is still known as today.

Much of what was being done in Iowa and in the association was being done in conjunction with Iowa State University. In 2001, ISU established a viticulture page on its website. That same year, Governor Vilsack of Iowa signed into legislation $75,000 per year for grape/wine promotion. While a small amount, this was one of the first times the state had stepped forward and acknowledged the importance of viticulture in Iowa. In 2003, it received its first portion for Iowa wine taxes.

As viticulture began to grow in Iowa, so did the membership in the Iowa Grape Growers Association. In 2001, it gained its 100th member, and by 2002, it had doubled that number. That same year, Michael White was appointed as a part-time employee at the ISU Extension office as its viticulture specialist. Eli Bergmeier was hired by the Golden Hills RC&D as a viticulture technician covering the entire state of Iowa. In November 2002, the Two Rivers Grape and Wine Cooperative registered in Iowa.

Governor Vilsack signed another piece of legislation in 2005 that allowed 5 percent of Iowa wine tax to be used by the Iowa Grape and Wine Development Commission in order to promote and support winery education. In its first year, the commission was granted $250,000. At a federal level in 2005, the U.S. Supreme Court struck down a law limiting interstate shipments of wine between states.

In 2005, viticulture was once again taking hold in Iowa, and in September, the first Iowa Wine Festival was held in Indianola, with about one thousand people in attendance. A second festival was held in Clear Lake the next month with about five hundred people in attendance.

The governor continued to listen to the needs of Iowa wineries and signed into legislation the exemption of native wineries from state food processing inspection in 2006. Around the same time, the Iowa Board of Regents approved the formation of the Midwest Grape and Wine Industry Institute at ISU.

In an effort to continue to serve the needs of wineries that were forming and growing in Iowa, the ISU Wine Quality Enology lab began accepting and analyzing samples from Iowa commercial winemakers in order to make better wines and to identify problems as they arose before they became larger issues. In 2008, the Iowa legislature allocated $50,000 to the ISU Midwest Grape and Wine Industry Institute.

A new—well actually old—cousin of wineries was given a chance to operate in Iowa once again. In July 2010, artisan distilleries were now able to produce, sell and have tastings of spirits, including vodka, brandy and whiskey.

By 2011, the number of wineries in the state of Iowa had grown significantly, and ninety-seven state licenses had been accepted by the Iowa Alcohol Beverage Division.

The Iowa Wine Growers Association established the Iowa Quality Wine Consortium (IQWC) in January 2012. Wines with the IQWC or IQ seal have passed a rigorous chemical and sensory panel test. IQWC wines are produced from a minimum of 75 percent Iowa-grown fruit. The IQ wines are produced from less than 75 percent Iowa-grown grapes, other fruits and/or other winemaking material.

In May 2016, the IWGA Winemaker and Cellarworker apprenticeship program began. Every year, more wineries are added to the rosters of IWGA. While the industry is not nearly at the size and scope it was in the early twentieth century, the interest in Iowa wines both within and outside the state continues to grow as wineries bring home multiple medals from national and international competitions. The world is taking notice of this once-proud grape state as a contender on the wine world stage once again.

BIBLIOGRAPHY

Amana Heritage Society. Oral History Interview No. 27, March 20, 1981.

———. Oral History Interview No. 40, March 28, 1982.

———. Oral History Interview No. 50, March 31, 1982.

———. Oral History Interview No. 59, April 29, 1982.

———. "The Wine Industry." Amana Community Schools Collection 68, Amana Heritage Society, Amana, Iowa, Box 1, Folder 1966, 1, 6.

Assignment Iowa with Mary Jane Odell. Iowa Public Broadcasting, 1977. Video recording, collection of the Amana Heritage Society.

Black Hawk. *Life of Black Hawk*. Originally published 1833. Reprinted often in various editions. Revised in 1882 with inauthentic embellishments; most modern editions restore the original wording.

Buckley, Jay H. *William Clark: Indian Diplomat*. Norman: University of Oklahoma Press, 2008.

Cedar Rapids Gazette. "Amana Winemakers: Old Art by Modern Methods." July 6, 1975.

———. "Winemaking Amana Style." June 18, 1985.

———. "Wine-Making at Amana." June 7, 1959.

Cedar Rapids Republican. "Red and Yellow Wine Poured into the Street Gutters; All Seven Amana Villages Have Abolished Booze." June 24, 1917.

Clemens, Gaycia. "Communal or Gemeinschaftliche Wineries." Unpublished paper.

Deemer, Lee. *Esther's Town*. Ames: Iowa State University Press, 1980.

Des Moines Sunday Register. "Amana Adds Wine Making to Activities." October 7, 1945.

DeVoto, Bernard. *The Year of Decision, 1846*. 1943. Repr., New York City: St. Martin's Griffin, 2000, 82–86.

Eby, Cecil. *"That Disgraceful Affair," the Black Hawk War*. New York: Norton, 1973.

Edmunds, R. David. *The Potawatomis: Keepers of the Fire*. Norman: University of Oklahoma Press, 1978.

Field, Homer H., and Hon. Joseph R. Reed. *History of Pottawattamie County, Iowa, from the Earliest Historic Times to 1907*. Vol. 1. N.p., n.d.

Flanders, Robert Bruce. *Nauvoo: Kingdom on the Mississippi*. Urbana: University of Illinois Press, 1965, 24–38.

Greene, John P. *Facts Relative to the Expulsion of the Mormons or Latter Day Saints, from the State of Missouri, under the "Exterminating Order."* Cincinnati, OH: R.P. Brooks, 1839.

Hall, John W. *Uncommon Defense: Indian Allies in the Black Hawk War*. Harvard University Press, 2009.

Hoehnle, Peter A. *Winemaking in the Amana Colonies*. Amana, IA: Wilrona, LLC, privately published, 2017.

Hoppe, Emilie. "Ackerman Family Creates New Home for Winery." *Willkommen* (Late Summer 2001).

———. "The Heart of Iowa's Growing Wine & Beer Industry." *Willkommen* (Autumn Holiday 2011).

———. "Les Ackerman Named Winemaker of the Year." *Willkommen* (Summer 2013).

———. *Seasons of Plenty: Amana Communal Cooking*. Ames: Iowa State University Press, 1994, 120.

"Indian Land Cessions in the United States, 1784 to 1894." A Century of Lawmaking for a New Nation: U.S. Congressional Documents and Debates, 1774–1875. Library of Congress, American Memory.

The Inspirationists, 1714–1932. London: Pickering and Chatto, 2015, 119.

Iowa Alcohol Beverage Division. www.iowaabd.com.

ISU Leopold Center. "Grape Expectations: A Food System Perspective on Redeveloping the Iowa Grape Industry." August 2002. www.leopold.iastate.edu/sites/default/files/pubs-and-papers/2002-08-grape-expectations-food-system-perspective-redeveloping-iowa-grape-industry.pdf.

Jung, Patrick J. *The Black Hawk War of 1832*. Norman: University of Oklahoma Press, 2007.

Kraus, George, and E. Mae Fritz. *The Story of an Amana Winemaker*. Iowa City, IA: Penfield Press, 1984.

Lankes, Frank J. *The Ebenezer Community of True Inspiration*. Gardenville, NY: privately published, 1949.

Leggett, Herbert Boyton. "Early History of Wine Production in California." *Wine Institute*, 1941.

Mattes, Joan. Amana Community Schools. Collection 68, Amana Heritage Society, Amana, Iowa, Box 1, Folder 1963, 1.

Mills, George. *A Judge and a Rope and Other Stories of Bygone Iowa*. Ames: Iowa State University Press, 1994.

Minutes of the Board of Trustees of the Amana Society. August 21, 1884.

———. September 2, 1884.

Neill, E.D. *The History of Minnesota: From the Earliest French Explorations*. Philadelphia: J.B. Lippincott Company, 1858, 400.

Nichols, Roger L. *Black Hawk and the Warrior's Path*. Arlington Heights, IL: Harlan Davidson, 1992.

———. *Warrior Nations: The United States and Indian Peoples*. Norman: University of Oklahoma Press, 2013.

Odegard, Peter H. *Pressure Politics: The Story of the Anti-Saloon League*. New York: Octagon Books, 1966.

Owens, Robert M. *Mr. Jefferson's Hammer: William Henry Harrison and the Origins of American Indian Policy*. Norman: University of Oklahoma Press, 2007.

Petersen, William. *The Annals of Iowa*. Vol. 1, *1863, With a Historical Introduction*. Iowa City, 1868.

Pinney, Thomas. *A History of Wine in America: From the Beginnings to Prohibition*. N.p., 1989.

Rettig, Lawrence L. *Gardening the Amana Way*. Iowa City: University of Iowa Press, 2013, 29.

Ruff, Henry. *Jakob Schumacher, Diary, 1876–1881*. Trans. by Henry J. Ruff, ed. by Peter Hoehnle. N.p., n.d.

———. Minutes of the Board of Trustees of the Amana Society, September 29, 1865.

———. Minutes of the Board of Trustees of the Amana Society, June 21, 1869.

———. Minutes of the Board of Trustees of the Amana Society, September 1, 1896.

———. Minutes of the Board of Trustees of the Amana Society, April 6, 1897.

———. Minutes of the Board of Trustees of the Eben-Ezer Society, Amana Church Archives.

Schwieder, Dorothy. *Iowa: The Middle Land.* Ames: Iowa State University Press, 1996, 212.

Shambaugh, Bertha M.H. *Amana: The Community of True Inspiration.* Iowa City: State Historical Society of Iowa, 1908, 186.

Strohman, James. *Amana Colonies Guide to Dining, Lodging and Tourism.* Ames: Iowa State University Press, 1997, 68–69, 70.

Trask, Kerry A. *Black Hawk: The Battle for the Heart of America.* New York: Henry Holt and Company, 2006.

USDA Farm Service Agency, www.fsa.usda.gov.

Webber, Phillip E. Minutes of the Board of Trustees of the Amana Society, May 2, 1911. Amana Heritage Society Archives.

———. Minutes of the Board of Trustees of the Amana Society, August 25, 1914.

———. Minutes of the Board of Trustees of the Amana Society, May 19, 1917.

White, Michael. "101 Iowa Grape & Wine Industry Facts." www.extension.iastate.edu/wine/files/page/files/101_facts_about_ia_grapes_n_wine_aug2015.pdf.

Whitney, Ellen M., ed. *The Black Hawk War, 1831–1832.* Vol. 1, *Illinois Volunteers*. Springfield: Illinois State Historical Library, 1970.

———. *The Black Hawk War, 1831–1832.* Vol. 2, *Letters & Papers, Part I, April 30, 1831–June 23, 1832.* Springfield: Illinois State Historical Library, 1973.

———. *The Black Hawk War, 1831–1832.* Vol. 2, *Letters & Papers, Part II, June 24, 1832–October 14, 1834.* Springfield: Illinois State Historical Library, 1975.

———. *The Black Hawk War, 1831–1832.* Vol. 2, *Letters and Papers, Part III, Appendices and Index*. Springfield: Illinois State Historical Library, 1978.

Zeller, John, research editor. *Behind the Badge: Stories and Pictures from the Des Moines Police Department.* Des Moines, IA: Peglow Art & Design Publishing, 1999.

INDEX

A

Ackerman Winery 82, 87, 108
Amana 63, 64, 65, 66, 68, 69, 70, 71, 73, 74, 78, 79, 81, 82, 83, 86, 87, 89, 90, 91, 105, 106, 108, 110
Amana Society 66, 78

B

Barney, Hiram 25, 26, 31, 33, 34, 35
Barney, Lewis 33, 34, 35, 38
basket press 83
Black Hawk 21, 22, 26, 27, 28, 29, 30, 109

C

Chief Keokuk 26
Clifton Vineyard 19
Colony Village Winery 90
Council Bluffs 24, 44, 45, 46, 47, 48, 49, 52, 57, 58, 62, 93, 99, 102
Council Bluffs Grape Growers Association 44, 45, 46, 48, 49, 50, 52, 54, 57, 58, 59, 61, 99

D

Davenport 15, 18, 19, 21, 111
Davenport, George 17, 18
Davenport, George L. 15, 17, 18, 19
Der Weinkeller (the Wine Cellar) 90
Des Moines 39, 48, 82, 101, 112, 113, 115

E

Edelweiss 103, 105, 106

F

Fox tribe 25

G

Grape Vine Winery 91

H

half-breed program 25, 26

K

Keokuk 22, 24

L

liquor 61, 74, 95, 96, 97
Little Amana Winery 89
L'oste Vineyard 19

M

Middle Amana 68, 81
Mormons 25

O

Old-Style Colony Winery 81, 82
Old Wine Cellar 89

P

pesticide 99
Prohibition 45, 57, 73, 78, 79, 94, 95

R

rhubarb 71, 105, 106

S

Sandstone Winery 89
Sauk 18, 25, 26, 27, 28, 31
St. Croix 103, 106

T

Tassel Ridge Winery 112
2,4-D 81, 98, 99, 100

W

White Cross Cellars 91
White Elk Vineyard 43
White Elk Winery 31
winery 59, 79, 81, 86, 87, 89, 90, 94, 97, 104, 105, 106, 107, 108, 109, 112, 113, 114, 116

ABOUT THE AUTHOR

John Peragine is a published author of thirteen books and has ghostwritten many others. He has written for the *New York Times*, Reuters and Bloomberg news as a journalist. John also writes for magazines such as *Writer's Digest*, *Wine Enthusiast*, *Acres USA Magazine* and *Grapevine Magazine*, just to name a few. John has been writing professionally since 2007, after working thirteen years in the field of social work. He was the piccolo player for the Western Piedmont Symphony for twenty-four years. John lives with his wife and children on the bluffs in Davenport, Iowa, overlooking the Mississippi River. When he is not writing, he is working with his grapes in the L'oste Vineyard.